D1648633

# MY AIN FOLK

# MY AIN FOLK
## An Easy Guide to
## Scottish Family History

Graham S. Holton and Jack Winch

TUCKWELL PRESS

First published in Great Britain in 1997 by
Tuckwell Press Ltd
The Mill House
Phantassie
East Linton
East Lothian EH40 3DG

Reprinted with corrections in 1998

© Graham Holton and Jack Winch 1997
All rights reserved

The right of Graham S. Holton and Jack Winch to be
identified as the authors of this work has
been asserted by them in accordance with the
Copyright, Design and Patent Act 1988.

ISBN 1 86232 024 1

A Catalogue record for this book is available on request
from the British Library

Typeset by Palimpsest Book Production Limited
Polmont, Stirlingshire

Printed and bound by
Caledonian, Bishopbriggs, Scotland

# CONTENTS

Introduction     vii

Illustrations     ix

1. The Whys and Wherefores     1
2. Relatively Easy?     13
3. Climbing the Tree     24
4. Storing the Information     34
5. Branching out:     40
   Historical Sources back to 1841
6. Digging Deeper: Sources before 1841     63
7. Writing it up     84
8. Widening the Net     91

Appendix A: Forms for recording Information     107
  1. Family Questionnaire     108
  2. Birth Certificate Details     112
  3. Marriage Certificate Details     113
  4. Death Certificate Details     114
  5. Census Details     115
  6. IGI Details     116
Appendix B: Useful Addresses     117
Further Reading and Sources     126
Index     145

# INTRODUCTION

This book has grown out of an interest in tracing their forebears, and filling out the history associated with them, shared by the two authors Graham Holton and Jack Winch. They have both pursued their family histories, which are quite different, over many years. The book encapsulates and distils that joint experience into a form that will assist both beginners and the more experienced in their own investigations.

It is based on a course in tracing family history which the two authors run for the Continuing Education Centre of the University of Strathclyde in Glasgow. Whilst the book focuses on Scottish Family History in the main, it has sections on English and Irish ancestry.

*My Ain Folk* aims to be easily accessible, yet comprehensive. It can be read from beginning to end, the order of the chapters relating to the way in which you might begin your researches. Thereafter, the chapters can act as sources of reference on particular aspects of family history research, equally suited to the beginner or the more experienced.

The survey of sources in Chapters 5 and 6 is divided up at the year 1841, but this is a rather arbitrary dividing line. The aim was to include, in Chapter 5, the main 'historical' sources (as opposed to 'genealogical' sources, which are dealt with in Chapter 3) for the period 1841 onwards, but you will find that many of these actually begin at an earlier date. Chapter 6 is intended to cover the most important 'genealogical' and 'historical' sources for the period before 1841, but here again, many of these continue beyond 1841. The reason for their inclusion in Chapter 6 is that they are more significant as sources for the earlier period than for the later.

The book includes a section on using computers to help in your investigations, and introduces you to that most recent of genealogical aids, the Internet. A list of Internet addresses is provided, which is as up to date as possible at the time of printing, but such addresses are rapidly changing. As far as possible, we have included resources such as searchable databases and listings of primary sources, rather than specific family histories. Many of the addresses have links to other sources of information on the Internet.

In order to try to provide more up to date information, we propose to maintain the following Internet addresses for this purpose:

http://www.lib.strath.ac.uk/family_history

http://www.strath.ac.uk/Departments/JHLibrary/fam.hl/.html

This list of useful addresses can also be found on the internet, with relevant links at:

http://www.strath.ac.uk/Departments/JHLibrary/fam.h2.html

The 'further reading and sources' list aims to include as many references as possible to useful reading and published sources for those tracing their Scottish ancestors. There is also a small selection of general works and works relating to English and Irish family history. Some of the items on specific topics in family history focus on England, but also have some relevance to Scotland. In general we have tended to exclude older works which have now been largely superseded, but in the area of computers and family history, since this is a relatively recent development, a fairly comprehensive coverage has been attempted.

Finally, we would like to express our thanks to the late Mr. Peter Vasey and other staff of the Scottish Record Office. Peter gave his very willing assistance by both discussing the relevant sources in the Scottish Record Office and subsequently reading and commenting upon sections of the text along with some of his colleagues.

Mrs. Margaret Harrison, Librarian of Jordanhill Library, University of Strathclyde, lent her assistance by giving advice on the parts of the book dealing with teachers and schools.

We should like also to express our thanks to anyone else who has assisted either knowingly or unknowingly in the preparation of this book.

Graham Holton and Jack Winch
Glasgow, May 1997

## ILLUSTRATIONS

(between pages 70 and 71)

1. Family tree of Campbells of Glenorchy
2. Pedigree search screen from the Personal Ancestral File (PAF)
3. General Register House
4. Historical Search Room, Scottish Record Office
5. West Register House
6. One of the 'Genuki' pages on the World Wide Web

CHAPTER ONE

# The Whys and Wherefores

'Why, oh why, do I want to research my family history?'
Have you ever stopped to think?

You may only have a hazy idea of your motives, or you
may have some very specific reason for embarking on this
'family history business'.

Maybe it is purely for the fun of it; of discovering
your 'roots', delving into the unknown. Where were
your ancestors born, where did they live, what were
their occupations and what sort of lives did they lead?
You may well, as many families do, have some family
tradition that a particular relative was present at some
historic event, or even left an unclaimed fortune! Such
stories have perhaps spurred you into action, in an
attempt to prove their truth or otherwise. Despite nat-
ural scepticism, there is very often a grain of truth in
such traditions but at the same time they are not usually 'the whole truth.'

## Family traditions?

Here is one amongst several stories in one of the authors'
families, part of which has been proven by means of several sources; according to 'family legend' a McArthur
ancestor was a ship's surgeon aboard the *Victory* at the
Battle of Trafalgar in 1805.

After some work, the author's descent from a Florence McArthur in Glasgow was traced, and some time later he discovered a substantial entry for her grandson, Dr. John Dougall, in *Who's who in Glasgow in 1909*. There was, of course, plenty of interesting information about John Dougall himself, including a photograph. However, the entry mentioned his relative 'Sir' Duncan McArthur, repeating the story that he had been aboard HMS *Victory* at Trafalgar. Finally, a copy of an article about Duncan was discovered in Glasgow City Archives, showing that he had in fact served on board the *Victory*, but about ten years before the Battle of Trafalgar. Also, although not actually knighted, he was awarded the C.B., one rank below that of knighthood. This Duncan was a brother of Florence and son of Duncan, a gardener in Glasgow.

Amongst the traditions in your 'family folklore' there may be claims to a relationship to an historical figure or to the nobility which again you will be keen to investigate further. We will return to descents from the nobility later.

### Tales of the unexpected?

In the course of your researches, you may uncover a totally unexpected relationship. This happened in the course of one of our own pieces of research, when, having located a great-great grandmother's death certificate, her mother's maiden name was found to be Munnings. As an interesting example of the unreliability of some sources, the mother's Christian name was recorded as Elizabeth, whereas when the great-great grandmother's baptism was traced, her mother turned out to be Sarah Green Munnings. Sarah was a sister of William Green Munnings, the grandfather of Sir Alfred Munnings, a famous painter, best known for his paintings of horses and a controversial President of the Royal Academy.

# Private detective work?

Family history research involves a considerable amount of detective work, often having been compared to piecing together a jigsaw, and this aspect can prove quite exciting. As family lines lead off in different directions you could find yourself researching the history of an area, an occupation or an industry with which your family was connected and as a result gaining new historical knowledge and insights. History can be given an added relevance when you know of your family's involvement. It becomes more personalised and has an added interest.

# Practical benefits?

Those of you with a more practical motive behind your interest may have found that for legal or religious reasons you are required to undertake some research into your family's past. Anyone claiming an hereditary title in the United Kingdom must provide genealogical proof to substantiate their claim. In some European countries, proof of nobility over a certain period of time ensured the right to tax exemptions and entry to the army or civil service at a minimum rank, and in some societies it has been necessary to show a family's high status to qualify for office. Although such needs may appear to apply mainly to the upper classes, the ordinary individual may also encounter similar needs. If an individual dies without leaving a will and has no known relatives, members of the family would be required to prove their relationship if they wished to inherit anything. Again, in medieval England, unfree tenants could not bring a case to court since they had no legal standing, but if they could prove a relationship to freemen, the case could go ahead. As a result, English medieval records contain genealogies of ordinary people recorded for this purpose.

Members of the Church of Jesus Christ of Latter Day Saints or Mormons, as they are usually known, have a religious motive behind their enthusiasm for genealogy. Mormons are required to trace as many as possible of their ancestors so that they can be baptised by proxy. They believe that only those baptised by a Mormon priest can achieve full salvation and that this can be done for dead relatives whom they believe would have become Mormons if they had had the opportunity. As a result, the Mormon Church has undertaken a vast amount of work in microfilming and inputting genealogical data to computer files. This has been of great benefit to genealogists throughout the world, and as you might expect, the Mormons now have an enormous storehouse of information which is contained in a huge underground library, near Salt Lake City, U.S.A. Some of the direct benefits of the work of the Mormons to other researchers such as ourselves will receive further mention in Chapter 3.

Genetics is to some extent related to the study of genealogy and it is worth remembering that all of our ancestors are important in creating us as individuals. You may often find genetics mentioned in the news, concerning either theories on the origins of man, or more controversially over the identification of specific genes which govern human characteristics such as the likelihood of cystic fibrosis. In the past, research has been undertaken into inherited diseases such as haemophilia and porphyria, and Sir Francis Galton (d.1911), the founder of the study of eugenics, tried to discover to what extent talent was inherited, by examining the genealogies of individuals with particular talent. The Bach family of musicians and composers could be claimed to be a good example of such inheritance.

## Importance of family history to other subjects

We would like to point out here that, although family history has an obvious interest for the reasons already mentioned, its importance reaches much further, into the fields of local, economic and social history and historical demography. If we take a magnifying glass to the whole expanse of history we see the local history of each area and then, with a stronger lens, the family history of those who make up each individual community. In focusing on the individuals within a community, family history can illuminate and bring new perspectives to a study of a particular locality. Whether of high or low status, the family about which we are gathering information played a role in local society which was probably similar to that played by other families of comparable status. You may have information on the type of life lived by a whole section of the community or perhaps facts about a particular occupation important in the area. These are the sort of details which a local historian will need in order to provide a representative picture of life in the locality concerned. Such information can also be drawn upon by economic and social historians working on a broader scale and, in particular, by those studying historical demography.

Notable in this field in England has been the Cambridge Group for the History of Population and Social Structure, in particular, Peter Laslett, R.S. Schofield and E. A. Wrigley. From the 1960s they have been studying records of specific English parishes and applying statistical methods in order to analyse the populations and thereby draw conclusions. They have studied literacy, by looking at the ability to sign marriage registers or other documents, and social structure from Census returns and other listings of inhabitants. The main procedures they have used, however, are aggregation and family reconstitution. Aggregation uses the total figures of baptisms, marriages and burials from parish registers and is a fairly quick means of analysing population trends. The types of information gained are: the growth or decline of population; baptism, marriage and burial rates; marital fertility rates; infant mortality rates; mobility of population and illegitimacy rates.

Family reconstitution, although a much slower method, allows a more detailed and accurate analysis. In this case, information is gathered from various sources about members of particular families in order to 'reconstitute' them. Calculations are then made to establish: age at marriage; age at burial; age at the end of marriage; length of marriage; age of mother at baptisms of children; interval between baptisms and number of children. This information tells us a lot about the sociology of the family at different times and in different places and, used together with data on the weather and harvest yields, the impact of epidemics and so on, can greatly increase our knowledge of the social and economic history of this country.

In the process of family reconstitution, the historical demographers are doing much the same as the family historian but for a large number of families in a parish. The conclusions which they draw can provide a context within which to place our own family. Was our family and its individual members unusual in the time and place in question or did they follow the normal pattern of family life? These are the sort of questions that we would like to answer and the methods and work of historical demographers may help us to do that.

Apart from the work of D.F. Macdonald, *Scotland's shifting population, 1770–1850* published in 1937, the population history of Scotland received little attention until the '70s, which saw the publication of *Scottish population history from the 17th century to the 1930s*, edited by Michael Flinn. Over the last few years there have been various research projects on the subject based at the Universities of Strathclyde, Aberdeen and Glasgow and some of the results have been published in *Glasgow, volume II: 1830 to 1912*.

# Genealogy in the past

Throughout the ages, genealogy has varied in importance, depending on place and period and for widely differing reasons. Genealogists in the Ancient World often traced the origins of a family or race back to gods and heroes. Genealogy helped to provide an extra unity to societies which emphasised kinship and demonstrated the necessary status which could entitle a family to an office, title or ownership of land. For example, Julius Caesar claimed descent from the Goddess Venus, through the Trojan Aeneas, while the Greeks Hippocrates and Aristotle both believed they were descended from Asclepius, the God of medicine. The Bible contains many genealogies tracing descents from Adam and Eve, and in both China and Japan in ancient times, family records were well maintained. Most Chinese families kept a Generation Book, usually updated about every thirty years, which recorded births, marriages and deaths along with other information about the families. The Japanese Government set up an office in 761 to record clan genealogies, and within a hundred years or so, more than 1,100 clans had been registered.

Medieval times saw the production of Norse sagas, Bede's 'Ecclesiastical history of the English people', the Anglo-Saxon Chronicle and Geoffrey of Monmouth's 'History of the kings of Britain', in all of which a great interest in genealogy is evident. Descents from Gods and heroes are numerous, but in most cases quite fictitious. In Scotland, the sennachies of the Highland clans were the bards who maintained the genealogical traditions of the clans. Their function was of great importance, not just from the fact that they could relate the ancestry of the members of the clan, linking them together and in some cases with the clan chief, but also because this information determined the rights of families to hold land and has been compared to the title deed in the feudal system.

From the sixteenth century, many genealogies were drawn up to prove the right to a coat of arms and to provide merchant and professional families with a high social status which they saw as important. By the end of the nineteenth century the production of genealogies was becoming much more scientific and the fabulous concoctions of the medieval genealogists were rejected. This reaction perhaps tended to go too far, and hopefully the study of genealogy today has reached a happy medium.

## Factors in tracing ancestry

Sir Anthony Wagner, in his book *English genealogy*, identified four factors governing the tracing of ancestry: status, record, name and continuity.

The status of a family in general affects the extent to which it appears in the records, and the status may be that of a noble family, of landowners, of holders of public office or of a merchant family. As we shall see, as a result of social mobility, there could be a considerable movement in and out of such families, and so you may find that your own family is at some periods much more easily traceable than at others.

The existence of records is obviously of vital importance in successfully tracing your family history. From time to time records may have been lost, damaged, destroyed or have been kept negligently. Some parish registers begin in the sixteenth century, others not until the eighteenth, which poses considerable problems for the genealogist.

Names, both Christian names and surnames, can range from the very common to the very unusual, and an unusual name or combination of names can make a tremendous difference in identifying the individual you are seeking. In city parishes with large numbers of baptisms, marriages and burials, there may be a number of persons of the same name registered round about the same date, given that the name is a fairly common one. On the other hand, if you are searching for an unusual name, there is a much greater chance of a correct identification. Customs for choosing Christian names, particularly in Scotland, can also lend a helping hand to the researcher.

Perhaps a few words on surnames may be helpful at this point. There are four main types of surnames: local names, relationship names, occupational names and nicknames. The local names could refer to a place of origin such as de Bruce, originally from Brius (now Brix) in Normandy, or a residence such as Wood or Marsh. Relationship names tend to be patronymics, giving the name of the father, such as Williamson or Robertson. Since Mac means son of, all the names beginning with Mac are of this type. At one time the patronymic changed with each generation, but eventually, many became established as surnames, and in the case of the Scottish clans the names beginning with Mac often refer to the individual regarded as the founder of the clan. Occupational names include Smith, Baker and Butcher while nicknames could, among other things, refer to appearance or qualities. Amongst these types of surnames are White, Long, Good and Savage.

Coming back to the factors involved in tracing ancestry, there is, finally, the factor of continuity. A family which has a continuous connection with one place is normally much easier to trace than one which moved about a lot. Movement from place to place often poses problems in family history research. It could take place on a small scale from parish to parish and was often more common than might be imagined. Movement within a ten-mile radius was very common in the past, but a move of a greater distance can be difficult for the family historian to trace. The greatest migration which affected the population as a whole was the movement from the country to the towns during the Industrial Revolution, particularly in the first half of the nineteenth century. Scotland also saw a great influx of Irish immigrants in the nineteenth century with the largest numbers settling in the Glasgow area but with significant numbers also in Edinburgh and Dundee. There have been other groups of immigrants in the past, but on a very much smaller scale. Continuity can also be evident in a long connection with a particular piece of land, an occupation or an institution. All such connections tend to improve the chance of successful research.

You are unlikely to be blessed with a combination of all these factors, and although your family may have been resident in one place for several centuries, you may have the misfortune to discover that the records are poor and only began relatively recently. Perhaps one of the other factors may provide extra assistance.

You may now be asking, what are the likely chances of success? Although you may hear of people who claim to be descended from Normans who came over with William the Conqueror, this is extremely unlikely. It seems that no one can prove a continuous descent in the male line from a companion of William at Hastings. There are a handful of very long descents in the male line which have been proved, a good example being the family of Arden, which is descended from Aelfwine, Sheriff of Warwickshire before 1066. In Scotland, the various branches of the family of Dundas can trace their ancestry back to Helias de Dundas, living in the early twelfth century. These descents are exceptional and probably on average you would be fortunate to trace back to the seventeenth century. You should certainly have a good chance of reaching the mid-eighteenth century.

## Social mobility

We have already mentioned, in passing, the question of noble descents and also social mobility in relation to a family's status. Social mobility in Britain was quite marked in contrast to other parts of Europe. It can involve a decline in status from one extreme to the other or may show movement up and down over the centuries. Some examples can illustrate this point well.

Having researched the Queen Mother's sixty-four ancestors in the seventh generation back, genealogists discovered that they included two dukes, three earls, a viscount, a baron, a duke's daughter, a marquess's daughter, an earl's daughter, a bishop's daughter, six country gentlemen, a director of the East India Company, a banker, three clergymen, the daughter of a Huguenot refugee, the landlord of the George Inn, Stamford, a London toyman and a London plumber. This research applied to ancestry, but examples can also be found in descents that have been researched. A peerage claim for the barony of Dudley, which was in abeyance from 1757 to 1914, brought to light the fact that the co-heirs, who were all descendants of King Henry VII (d.1509), consisted of a butcher, a gamekeeper, a tollgate keeper, a baker's wife and a tailor's wife.

One of the authors' ancestry provides an interesting example of social mobility. The author's branch of the Holton family moved to Scotland in the 1880s when his great-grandfather, then working as a commercial traveller, settled in Glasgow. He began his working life as a hosiery warehouseman and came from a family of farmers and butchers in Suffolk. His maternal grandfather, Anthony Hicks, had also been a farmer, but Anthony's mother, Sarah Timperley, although her immediate ancestors were Suffolk farmers, was the third generation in descent from Thomas Timperley, Lord of the Manor of Hintlesham. This family was for several generations closely associated with the Mowbray and Howard Dukes of Norfolk, and William Timperley actually married Margaret Howard, an illegitimate daughter of Thomas Howard, 3rd Duke of

Norfolk, in the early sixteenth century. The 3rd Duke, who was a major figure in the Court of Henry VIII, was descended, through the Mowbrays, from Thomas of Brotherton, the second son of King Edward I. If you do happen to prove a connection with a royal family, quite amazing ancestors can be traced. For example, Edward I was descended from William the Conqueror, St. Margaret of Scotland and the Emperor Charlemagne, while his second wife, Margaret of France, the mother of Thomas of Brotherton, numbered the Byzantine Emperor Constantine VII and Charlemagne amongst her ancestors.

We hope that, by way of introduction, this chapter has given you some background: firstly, on the history and uses of genealogy and the importance of family history to other historical studies; and secondly, on various factors which will affect the course of your own researches. Now let's start on research in earnest.

CHAPTER TWO

# *Relatively Easy?*

If you're setting out on the trail of tracing your ancestors
and collecting the history of your family together, the first
step should really be to try to gather as much information
as possible that you already know, or that other family
members know. You may find that information readily, or
you may find that it is tucked away in the recesses of
someone's mind, or in the depths of some relative's cup-
board or attic.

It would be possible to work back, just simply knowing
your own name and your date of birth, but this would be
a very clinical way of working. You could miss out on the
really interesting 'flesh' to be put on the 'bones' of
genealogy, the warmth and humour of family life, the
anecdotes about the characteristics of members of previous generations.

## The first source of information should really be yourself and family members

This is an extremely important first step – to try to gather
and collate all information from the living relatives to
whom you can gain access.

You may be surprised at how much genealogical information is stored in families, once you start to probe a bit
further. You may know a surprising amount yourself,

when you start to formalise, or organise that information. Other family members, especially maiden aunts, usually have access to records, certificates, photographs, family recollections, rumours and scandals which we don't!

## When should you start?

There is really no time like the present! You should be prepared to take any suitable opportunity to talk to members of the older generations within your family to talk about their brothers and sisters, parents, aunts, uncles and cousins and take careful note of what they have to tell you. If you delay, then members of the older generation may well have departed, taking all the gems of personal detail about your ancestors with them, never to be recovered!

Of course, you will have to approach the matter with a great deal of tact – if you suddenly ask a maiden aunt that you haven't bothered with for the last twenty years to give you all the most intimate details about the family, to hand over certificates and photographs at the first meeting, you are unlikely to achieve anything apart from instant suspicion of your motives, and a permanent refusal to have any further dealings with you! You must try to establish a relationship of mutual trust, genuine interest and concern. This will take time and effort, but can pay huge dividends in the longer run.

## What kind of material are you looking for?

**Names**
**Dates**
**Places**
**Occupations**

These may take the more official form of Birth Certificates, Marriage Certificates, Death Certificates.

However, other less formal, or recollected verbal information is worth recording, but should not be accepted as absolutely accurate.

Further information, of a less cold statistical nature, is very useful as you build up a picture of your family history, to find out what 'made your forebears tick', to trace shared characteristics through the generations, etc. Some headings (though this is not an exhaustive list) could be:

**Appearance**
**Characteristics**
**Habits**
**Motives**
**Odd Sayings**
**Family Legend(s)**
**Old Photographs**
**Memorial Cards**
**Indentures**
**Granny's Birthday Book**
**School Reports**
**Army Rolls of Honour**
**Family Bible**

## How should I approach the gaining of information from relatives?

This has to be done carefully, sympathetically, and tactfully! Don't over-tire the elderly. Talk about people in the way the relative will know them – your grandmother should be discussed as 'your cousin Sadie', etc. Don't press for specific dates, but try to relate to world, national, local or personal events, e.g. 'The War', or 'when you were at school', or 'before Jimmy left home'. Perhaps an unobtrusive tape-recording could be taken, rather than be scribbling notes and have to ask for repetition of some detail.

## Some keynotes of success

Don't be in a hurry to go somewhere else, or over-stay your welcome! Try to make them relax, and be friendly rather than harass and offend. Be kind and thoughtful to the 'attentive daughter', be kind to any pets! You want them to feel that you are genuinely interested in the other people and them, rather than trying to get hold of the family silver! Make a point of recording as much information as possible, including those details that may not seem important at the time, but might turn out to be very helpful later.

## A good strategy?

Don't go to visit a relative with a view to gaining all the information you can, without offering anything in return! This will immediately arouse suspicion, and you should try to add some information to which you have access, even if it's simply the latest news and pictures of your branch of the current generation.

Some possible items to take with you could be:

**family photographs**
**mystery pictures**
**a small tape-recorder?**
an incomplete, or **outline family tree**
(leaving room for
discussion on details)
sometimes a **well-trained spouse** or **offspring**
can be helpful

Leave behind, during your visit:
animals (unless you know they are
specifically wanted)
boisterous children
restless teenagers
a restless spouse

## A system for recording this information

You may or may not decide that taking a small tape-recorder would be suitable for recording information gained during your visit with an elderly relative. No matter what you decide, it is vital that you record in some permanent, readable form all the information that you have already, or have gained during this 'interview'. An example of a form which should cover all the potential areas of interest is illustrated in Appendix A – The Family Questionnaire Form.

This could be posted to a relative, or could simply be used as a structure to record the results of your meeting. It is important to say at this point that, although the bare facts of names, places and dates are very important to build up the structure or skeleton of your family history, the anecdotes about relatives are much more enlivening to your new-found interest. It can be quite exciting to hear of the eccentricities, pet likes and dislikes, or sense of humour of someone who previously had just been a name on a yellowing certificate or the subject of a rather staid, sepia photograph.

Information about the existence of other sources of family knowledge, such as a Family Bible, or news of a distant cousin also interested in the family, can open up new vistas of possibilities.

At this stage, you shouldn't worry that there are more blanks than completed spaces. It is very likely that the information which you already have, or have been given isn't 100% accurate.

Later on, in Chapter 3, we will show you that there are ways to use your possibly inaccurate information to lead you to reliable sources of accurate dates, etc.

Another possible means of recording information is an individual record of significant details about one particular relative or ancestor. Depending upon your preference, you may find this easier to handle during an interview, but it has the limitation that it does not allow for extra, exciting anecdotes to be added, but caters solely for the bare statistical bones of the individual concerned. Here are some broad headings which could be used:

**First names:**
**Surname:**
**When born:**
**Where born:**
**When baptised:**
**Where baptised:**
**Father's Name:**
**Father's Occupation:**
**Mother's Name:**
**Parents' Date of Marriage:**
**Parents' Place of Marriage:**
**Date of Marriage:**
**Date of Death:**
**Place of Death:**
**Cause of Death:**

Whatever method you decide to use for keeping your records, it is very important to be methodical and well-organised. The best time to get into the habit is right away, at the start. So many of us involved in family history research have, in our enthusiasm, jotted down notes on different subjects and from different sources all in the same notebook. This soon makes it very much more difficult to locate information than it need be, and it takes a great deal of work to reorganise the data at a later stage. With some careful planning at the outset, this situation can be avoided.

## Means of displaying a family tree

*The Drop Line Chart*

You will probably already have seen the most common form of graphically displaying a family tree – in the form of a 'tree' with the twigs and branches decked out with leaves, each leaf representing a family member.

The links back to the common ancestor are shown moving back through the twigs to the larger branches and finally to the trunk. This kind of tree can most commonly be seen in museums representing the genealogy of aristocratic or royal families. (See Plate no.1)

However, a simpler form of this can be seen in the Drop Line Chart.

The oldest generation is shown at the top of the chart, with succeeding generations branching out lower down the chart, with links moving downwards normally through 'marriage', which is indicated by an 'equals' (=) sign. The same generations can be seen side-by-side along the same row on the chart. Sometimes if there are many generations and large families, the chart can demand very wide paper or extremely small, cramped writing. It may be impossible to arrange for all those of the same generation to appear on the same row. The details you include could vary widely from the basic names with dates of birth or baptism, and death or burial to more elaborate entries with places of birth, marriage and death, date of marriage, occupations, etc.

*The Birth Brief*

The Birth Brief begins on the left-hand side of the page, with one individual. As you proceed to the right, you move back in time to the parents, grandparents, great-grandparents and so on, with each generation of ancestors

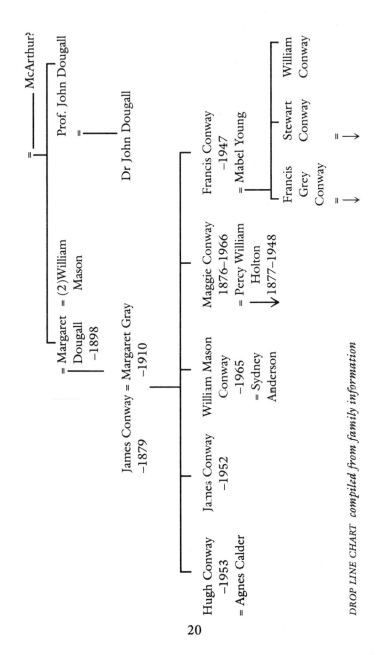

*DROP LINE CHART compiled from family information*

arranged in columns. It is possible to have a number of these charts, each beginning with a different individual, to record various lines of ancestors. The limitation is, of course, that it does not accommodate brothers, sisters and their descendants, as the Drop Line Chart does.

## The Circular Tree

Like the Birth Brief, this can be a useful starting tool for building up the framework of a family tree. It is limited in that it does not show brothers and sisters, but only parents of one child. You can think of it as a cross-section of a tree-trunk, with succeeding rings radiating outwards.

Normally, you would start out with yourself in the central 'core' of the circle or 'trunk' and move outwards to your mother and father in the next 'shell', then their parents in the succeeding shell, etc. . . etc. A number of these charts can be used, with different interesting individuals forming the central core.

This will suffice as a starting place to record your information. As your 'research' starts to build up, we will see that increasingly there are commonly available information technology tools which will help you to keep track of the vast quantities of interesting detail which you will accumulate surprisingly quickly, without resorting to pencil and rubber, screwing up paper and rewriting vast tracts of information.

As a worthwhile side-effect, the space taken up by your family history hobby will be smaller – no small benefit in a busy home!

Good hunting – remember, family history begins at home!

8 Henry Thomas WINCH
born
where Queenborough, Kent
when married
died

9 Margaret? Thomson? RAMSAY
born Newhaven?
where
died ?

10 Robert MESSER
born
where
when married
died

11
born
where
died

12
born
where
when married
died

13
born
where
died

14
born
where
when married
died

15
born
where
died

4 John Ramsay WINCH
born c 1883
where Queenborough, Kent
when married 1906
died 1963

5 Euphemia MESSER
born c1875
where Edinburgh
died 1965

6 Theophilus HULSON
born
where
when married
died c.1923

7 Minnie ?
born Plymouth?
where
died

2 Henry Thomas WINCH
born 7 February 1910
where Newhaven, Midlothian
when married 26 May 1951
died 16 February 1997

3 Minnie HULSON
born 3 March 1915
where Birmingham
died 6 December 1984

1 John Ramsay WINCH
born 1 April 1952
where Johnstone,
Renfrewshire
when married 6 July 1979
died
Aileen Anne Elizabeth
DUNN
Name of husband or wife

*BIRTH BRIEF compiled from family information*

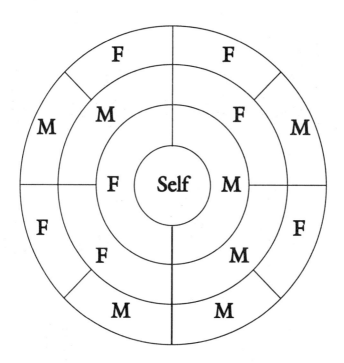

CIRCULAR TREE

CHAPTER THREE

# Climbing the Tree

In this chapter we seek to help you to find more information about your family history, once you have exhausted (perhaps literally!) all the sources you have available in your family. At this stage the next step is to look into the documentary evidence available in official documents. One store of information is the most important for the intending family history researcher. That store, New Register House at the east end of Princes Street, Edinburgh, contains the official Scottish Civil Registers, the Census returns for 1841 to 1891 and the 'Old' Parish Registers. In this chapter we shall look at the different kinds of information that we can glean from the first two categories of records. We will come back to the Parish Registers in Chapter 6.

## Births, Marriages and Deaths since 1855

Just after your own birth, if it occurred in Scotland, when all the usual negotiation had taken place about what you were to be called, one of your parents probably went along to the local Registrar and fed your details into their system ('registering the birth'). A very similar system applies to marriages, whether the ceremony is carried out in a church or in a Registry Office, and also to deaths.

Since 1 January 1855 in Scotland, the state has assumed responsibility for the logging of the births, marriages and deaths of its citizens. The outcome of all this bureaucracy has been that a vast store of all the original entries since then has been indexed, maintained and made relatively accessible to you, as a member of the general public, for a reasonable fee.

Before we proceed to tell you of the procedure for gaining access to this treasure-trove of information, we will give you a few notes on what each type of certificate contains, and what to look out for when you get to look at the actual entries.

The *Birth Certificate* will give you, in addition to the details you already know about the person's name and sex:

• the date and place of birth – even down to the time of the baby's delivery. You should make special note of the address – later on when we look at Census returns, you will see that it can be a link to other interesting information.

• the parents' details – names, the father's occupation, the mother's maiden name, and the really valuable information about the date and place of the parents' marriage.

• the name of the informant – this is not normally of importance as it is usually the father or mother. However, if it is not, take a note of it as it may point to a relative, which can come in useful in later research.

If you happen to have a birth in 1855, you have struck lucky as it will provide you with information about the number of other children of the marriage at the time of the birth, together with the age and birthplace of the father and mother. Because of the burden of collecting this extra information, this practice was, unfortunately for the family historian, dropped after one year! The reaction against this was particularly sharp between 1856 and 1860, as birth certificates did not include details of the parents' marriage. However, this valuable information was reintroduced in 1861.

The *Marriage Certificate* will be even more fruitful as it contains information about two people. The information it will provide is as follows:
• where and when the marriage took place – if the ceremony was a religious one, it will tell you by which rites it was performed. This is not something to gloss over – it may point to a family tradition of churchgoing which could open up other sources of information later on.
• the name, occupation, 'condition' (bachelor or widower), age and address of the bridegroom. Additionally it provides the name and occupation of the father, and the name and maiden name of the mother – this is absolutely vital information to take a step back to the previous generation in your family tree.
• the equivalent details for the bride.
• the names of the witnesses to the signing of the marriage register. Most of the time this will be of little practical use, but take a note of them as it could be a clergyman, a friend, or a relative of the bride or 'groom – you never know when this will provide a key to your later researches.

The Scottish *Death Certificate* is a very valuable document in building up a family tree, unlike its English counterpart. It will tell you:
• the name and occupation of the person whose death has been registered. Sometimes this occupational information is important as it may have changed from the earlier entries in the children's birth certificates, marriage certificate, etc. Of course, if the deceased was well on in years, the informant may well not be too clear about the actual occupation.
• marriage details – again this is valuable information, especially where it refers to a marriage other than the one you had known about previously.
• where the death occurred – when this happens away from home, the regular address is provided, except for the period between 1856 and 1860. Such addresses should

be noted, both from the point of view of simply knowing where the people lived, and to allow you to access Census information at a later stage in your research.

• the person's age – not always accurate, but can be a reasonable guide to enable you to trace a birth entry in the registers.

• the names of both parents, and also the occupation of the father and maiden name of the mother. This information is the vital link which is missing from the English Death Certificate, and can enable you to take the all-important step backwards in your family tree. However, again dependent upon the age of the deceased, such names and occupations can sometimes be less than accurate.

• the cause of death – can be a bit technical, but worth recording. Sometimes the duration of the illness is also mentioned.

• the signature of the informant – the name of the person notifying the death can be more valuable for the family history researcher than the names of the informant on other certificates. It can help you to assess the reliability of the information, as referred to earlier. Further, it can provide useful genealogical information. For instance, if a Janet Messer (maiden name Robertson) has a death certificate signed by Thomas Meikle, brother-in-law, you can deduce that she has at least one sister, who had married a man called Thomas Meikle – not too bad for a small column at the end of a death certificate!

### The Census Records, 1841 to 1891

Just as the state had taken over responsibility for keeping track of births, marriages and deaths since 1855, it also became concerned with keeping details of the entire population and keeping track of its whereabouts. Since 1801 in Scotland, every ten years a census of the population has been taken, with the exception of 1941. However, only the statistical details have generally been retained for the censuses from 1801 to 1831, and therefore they are not of much use to the family historian.

The full returns for every household for the six censuses from 1841 to 1891 are available for inspection on micro-film at New Register House in Edinburgh on payment of the usual fee. Later census returns will not be made available to the general public until they are 100 years old, as they may contain some information about a living person which they would not wish to be released publicly. Increasingly, in order to make access easier, local libraries are obtaining copies related to their own parts of the country.

Census returns perhaps hold the greatest amount of information for the ancestor hunter, but searching through can be difficult. If your family lived in a small village where there were few inhabitants, finding your ancestors may be relatively easy. On the other hand, if they lived in a town or city, it could take an hour or two to find them, as they are not indexed by inhabitants' names, and only the larger towns and cities have a street index.

However, the 1881 Census now has a name index, arranged by counties on microfiche, and the 1891 Census has a computerised name index.

## What are the kinds of information you can glean from census returns?

In 1841, the census asked for a limited amount of infor-mation – names, approximate ages rounded down to the nearest five years, occupations, and whether the person was born in the county or not. For those under the age of 15, allegedly exact ages are given.

In 1851, questions being asked were names, relation-ships to the person designated as 'head of the household', precise ages and the actual parish of birth, if in Scotland.

By the time we reach 1891, a number of extra and

quite revealing questions were being asked, such as the ability to speak Gaelic, the number of rooms being shared by families, and evidence of disabilities.

The big benefit which the census returns bring to the family history researcher is to provide complete or partially complete family groupings in the one place. This could enable you to find brothers and sisters and perhaps other relatives. However, the absence of one expected person is no guarantee that they are deceased – they could have been away from home on business or staying with a friend on that particular census night. The census return will also provide you with information on the social circumstances of your ancestors. Don't neglect to take a look at the details of the neighbours. It may be useful to note down who is sharing a front door, or a close, with your ancestors, or living on the neighbouring farm. Census returns can tell you a lot about the activities of a locality.

### Some pitfalls?

One drawback of census returns is that you must know exactly where your family was living on that one night once every ten years, and you may end up on a long and perhaps fruitless search if your family was quite mobile. The numbering of streets was sometimes a bit disorganised, and different census enumerators could show different standards of care in noting down street numbers.

Here is an example of a census return from our own research:

**(Census for North Leith, 1881 – CEN 1881, 692(1))**
**26 James Place, Newhaven**

| Name | Position | Status | Age | Occupation | Birthplace |
|------|----------|--------|-----|------------|------------|
| John Ramsay | Head | Married | 48 | Fisherman | born Newhaven |
| Maryann Ramsay | Wife | | 40 | | born Newhaven |
| John Ramsay | son | | 22 | Fisherman | born Newhaven |
| William Ramsay | son | | 4 | scholar | born Newhaven |

| Street | Name | Relation | Status | Age | Occupation | Birthplace | Rooms |
|---|---|---|---|---|---|---|---|
| Williamsburgh 1 | HEANEY, Rosean | Head | Widow | 50 | | Ireland | 2 |
| Williamsburgh 1 | HEANEY, Peter | Son | Unmarried | 26 | Gardener | Renfrew-shire Houston | |
| Williamsburgh 1 | HEANEY, James | Son | Unmarried | 24 | Engineer Patternmaker | Renfrewshire Houston | |
| Williamsburgh 1 | HEANEY, Sarah | Daughter | Unmarried | 19 | Milliners Shopwoman | Renfrewshire Houston | |
| Williamsburgh 1 | HEANEY, Alexander Son | Unmarried | 15 | | Apprentice Mill Mecharic | Stirling-shire Baldernock | |
| Williamsburgh 1 | CHALMERS, Alexander | Head | Married | 34 | Wood Sawyer | Fife-shire Markinch | 2 |
| Williamsburgh 1 | HARKNESS, Isabella | Wife | Married | 34 | | Ayr-shire Kirkoswald | |
| Williamsburgh 1 | CHALMERS, William | Son | | 8 | Scholar | Renfrew-shire Paisley | |
| Williamsburgh 1 | CHALMERS, Jessie M K | Daughter | | 7 | Scholar | Renfrew-shire Paisley | |
| Williamsburgh 1 | CHALMERS, James | Son | | 5 | Scholar | Renfrew-shire Paisley | |
| Williamsburgh 1 | CHALMERS, Catherine Herc | Daughter | | 2 | | Renfrew-shire Paisley | |
| Williamsburgh 1 | CHALMERS, Isabella Harkness | Daughter | | 1m | | Renfrew-shire Paisley | |
| Williamsburgh 1 | GANSON, Elizabeth | Head | Widow | 54 | Housekeeper | Ireland | 3 |
| Williamsburgh 1 | GANSON, William | Son | Unmarried | 19 | Army Militia Staff | Renfrew-shire Paisley | |
| Williamsburgh 1 | GANSON, George | Son | Unmarried | 17 | Tailor's Apprentice | Renfrew-shire Paisley | |
| Williamsburgh 1 | JACK, Kate | Daughter | Married | 20 | Warehouse Worker | East India British Subject | 3 |
| Williamsburgh 1 | JACK, James | Son in Law | Married | 24 | Tailor | Renfrew-shire Paisley | |
| Williamsburgh 1 | JACK, Maggie | Grand Daughter | | 3 | | Renfrew-shire Paisley | |
| Williamsburgh 1 | JACK, George | Grand Son | | 1 | | Renfrew-shire Paisley | |
| Williamsburgh 1 | SHAW, David | Head | Married | 53 | Power Loom Tenter | Renfrew-shire Neilston | 3 |
| Williamsburgh 1 | SHAW, Mattie | Wife | Married | 52 | Power Loom Tenters | Renfrew-shire Paisley | |
| Williamsburgh 1 | SHAW, David | Son | Unmarried | 28 | Wool Cloth Miller | Renfrew-shire Paisley | |
| Williamsburgh 1 | SHAW, Robert | Son | Unmarried | 24 | Packing Box Maker | Renfrew-shire Paisley | |
| Williamsburgh 1 | SHAW, Margaret | Daughter | Unmarried | 21 | Housekeeper | Renfrew-shire Paisley | |
| Williamsburgh 1 | SHAW, William | Son | Unmarried | 19 | Flesher | Renfrew-shire Paisley | |
| Williamsburgh 1 | SHAW, Mary | Daughter | Unmarried | 17 | Thread Mill Worker | Renfrew-shire Paisley | |
| Williamsburgh 1 | SHAW, Jessie | Daughter | Unmarried | 15 | Thread Mill Worker | Renfrew-shire Paisley | |
| Williamsburgh 1 | SHAW, Hepsey | Daughter | | 12 | Scholar | Renfrew-shire Paisley | |
| Williamsburgh 1 | SHAW, John | Son | | 10 | Scholar | Renfrew-shire Paisley | |

This Newhaven census entry revealed a hitherto unknown son, aged four. There is also the possibility that this was actually a grandson, an illegitimate son of one of the daughters of the family, as such arrangements to cover up a family 'disgrace' were not unknown at the time.

The interesting social background provided by the detail contained in the 1891 census can be seen from the extract on page 30 from one address.

Amongst other things, the living conditions, particularly of the Shaw family – ten people living in a three-roomed house – are worthy of note, as an interesting insight into the social history of the area in which your ancestors were living.

### How do you make use of New Register House?

New Register House is normally open between the hours of 0900 and 1630, from Monday to Friday, apart from the fairly usual public holidays. A comprehensive instruction leaflet on making use of the facilities is produced every year (leaflet S1), which gives up-to-date details of charges and procedures for searching amongst the records available to the general public. Having paid your fee, you will be allocated a desk, complete with computer terminal, microfilm/fiche reader and instructions. You will not be permitted to write in pen, as this can permanently damage the delicate original records. For similar reasons, no smoking or drinking is allowed within the building, but there are plenty of refreshment places of all descriptions within a very short walk. The public search room is located under the dome, and it is a bright, airy place to spend a day searching the records.

Preparation before you go is essential! You should try to think out a number of lines of enquiry before you go, in order that you can make the fullest use of your valuable day beside the records. We would recommend taking a notebook, or loose-leaf binder, filled with some of the skeletal forms we suggest using (Appendix A).

The indexes of births, marriages and deaths are now all computerised, while the 1881 Census index is on microfiche and the 1891 Census index is on computer. The instructions for using these systems are fairly simple, and shouldn't prove too daunting for anyone! You can carry out a search for a particular birth, marriage or death over all Scotland or restricted to certain areas. These certificates are available on microfiche, whereas the actual census records are on microfilm.

It is worth noting that there are Registrar's Offices in Glasgow and Dundee, which give public access to the computer index of the Civil Registers. However, the microfiche copies of the actual entries held there cover, in the Glasgow Office, the area which used to be called Strathclyde Region, and in the Dundee Office, Dundee and Angus (for the earlier period). These offices also provide access to the 1891 computerised Census Index. There are plans to make a lot of the information stored in New Register House available through the Internet.

### The International Genealogical Index (the IGI)

The Church of Jesus Christ of the Latter Day Saints (the Mormons), whose headquarters is in Salt Lake City, USA, has developed an International Genealogical Index. Although their work was carried out for the purpose of their own religious belief in the desirability of baptising all people, even retrospectively after death, according to the rites of their own church, it incidentally provides a most valuable source of information for the family history researcher.

A huge amount of information about births, baptisms and marriages in the United Kingdom is available on microfiche or CD-ROM prepared by the Mormon

Church. Details of deaths and burials are not included. This collection (the IGI) can be accessed at their family history libraries, but it is also available at many local public libraries, which makes it a very useful facility. The CD-ROM version called Family Search, can be read by computer and this allows the information to be accessed much more quickly than from microfiche, and restricted searches are carried out automatically. The genealogical information on the IGI has been transcribed from the original sources, mainly the Old Parish Registers, which were accessed through New Register House by the Mormon Church. It has to be borne in mind, however, that there can be transcription errors and that the information is not so complete as in the original records – only the names of the parties directly involved are included (bride and 'groom for a marriage; child and parents for a birth or baptism), together with the registration district.

For England and Wales, the coverage is less complete than that for Scotland, as the information had to be collected from a wide variety of County Record/Archive Offices and from parishes which were sometimes reluctant to permit access to their records.

Nevertheless, the IGI provides a useful source at least for preliminary investigations which can be followed up by more rigorous searching in the original official records. The individual fiche relate to counties, within which they are in alphabetical order of surname. Births, baptisms and marriages are all mixed in together.

The Mormon Church's Family History Libraries hold not only the IGI, but also copies of many other records such as Census returns and the Old Parish Registers. So if you live near one of these libraries, it could be well worth a visit at an early stage. It may be necessary to book a time in advance, but there is no charge and you may find some useful information before moving on to the original sources in Edinburgh.

CHAPTER FOUR

# Storing the Information

Having carried out some research into your family history at home, from relatives, at New Register House and local libraries, you will very soon accumulate quite a considerable quantity of detailed information. Unless you have a systematic way of storing that information, it can very easily become confused and you can misunderstand the links and relationships. It's amazing how quickly important details can be lost or mislaid, especially if you rely on memory alone.

In this chapter we hope to illustrate the pros and cons of some ways of storing the harvest of your research, in order that you can keep it secure, yet gain ready access to update your family tree in the light of your latest research results.

As a general rule, you should always clearly distinguish between the information you have found in the original sources and the information you have built up based on these sources. The source material should be stored quite separately from your conclusions.

## Paper records

You can, of course, simply write the information down in a notebook. This is, naturally, an improvement on memory, supplemented by notes on scraps of paper. The difficulty which can arise is that, with further investigation, details can be changed, expanded and deleted. An improvement might be to store information on individuals by means of a sorted card-index system. This would allow for new individuals to be inserted in chronological or alphabetical order, and for additional notes to be added to individual cards.

## Keeping track by computer

The greatest, and most significant, advantage of using a computer system to assist in the maintenance of your family history research is that many different types of information – narrative, dates, relationships, illustrations, family trees, etc. – can be stored in the one compact space – namely on one computer system with perhaps a number of floppy disks. Using other more traditional means of storage, a considerable amount of space may be needed to keep your information, which can cause some ill-feeling amongst the living members of your family tree!

There are some aspects of your family tree that can never be stored on a computer system. Naturally, original certificates, photographs and papers still need to be stored, preferably in a secure and fireproof cabinet. Though the making of copies can never supplant the thrill of finding and retaining original documents, it is, however, possible to 'scan' copies of the original photographs and documents and store them as 'graphics' files on disk.

In the very gradual process of building up the 'picture' of your family history, the possibility of storing incomplete information which can be added to in a piecemeal fashion, without the need for a complete rewrite of the information is one of the main strengths of computer use for this purpose. There is the additional benefit that paper copies of the information can be printed out whenever you require, without having to arrange for photocopying or storing large quantities of duplicated paper records.

## Special Genealogical Software

There are a number of pieces of software specifically designed for the purpose of family history research. Many of these are produced primarily for profit-making purposes, can be quite expensive and are of variable quality. Many are produced to suit one system only, such as for a PC or for a Macintosh and so are very machine-dependent.

One system which has been developed for a number of different computer systems, is relatively comprehensive, is widely used internationally and is relatively cheap is the Personal Ancestral File System (PAF), produced by the Church of Jesus Christ of the Latter Day Saints, the Mormon Church. It is produced for religious purposes and has a number of additional features which need not be used. However, it is very useful for the genealogist, and performs most of the functions that you would be seeking. In the latest version, trees can be printed out, family records can be kept, details of individuals kept, narrative notes made – all in the context of a family 'database', with all the relationships defined that will allow you to search back and forwards through the generations, and across any particular generation. It is possible to print out any of the information stored on the PAF system.

Another feature is the Research Data Filer, which allows you to keep a catalogue of original documents on disk (as a Document File), and moreover to store data extracted from original documents (as a Data file). For example, Document No.1 in your Document File might be baptisms in the Parish of Govan for 1700–1800. All the entries you have extracted from this source would be stored in your Data File, with a reference to Document

No.1. These files could be searched, sorted and printed in various ways.

This PAF system has the added advantage, because of its widespread use, that you can share information easily with another researcher of your family who has access to the PAF system.

## *Word processing*

A normal wordprocessing system of any variety with which you are familiar is of enormous value to you in the pursuit of building up the narrative of your family history. You can write a partially complete narrative, and return to it with amendments and additions at any time as your investigations proceed. In the case of the wordprocessing software produced in the last five years or so, it is possible to include pictures (or graphics) which can help to enliven your narrative, and to save the illustrated narrative as a wordprocessed file on disk. If you have old photographs, rather than stick them on to your page, it is possible to use a 'scanner' attached to the computer which will copy them in a suitable form for storage along with your text as part of your wordprocessed file. Frequently it will be possible to enhance the scanned image if the original is somewhat faded. This then allows you to keep the precious original photographs safely filed away for posterity.

## *Databases*

If, for example, you have lists of census details which may be connected with your family, it will be of value to put them into a database. The fields of the database are the different columns in the census enumeration sheet, such as name, relationship to head of household, age, marital status, occupation, etc. Your collection can then be browsed through, searched, put into different orders and printed out in the order you wish. Another effective use of a database would be to store information which you have gathered from the International Genealogical Index (IGI).

## Audio cassette recording

Recollections of an elderly relative can be a rich source of family history, forming a living link with past generations. It is just possible that by this means you may be in touch with a personal recollection of an ancestor who was born 150 years ago. Recollections may be more colourful, when recorded as they were actually stated to you – they may be in a dialect which is fast disappearing, the narrator may mimic the way in which the story was originally told, and a whole lot of 'narrative colour' can be added to an otherwise fairly sterile piece of family history.

## Video recording

### Local history

If you are able to visit the area from which your ancestors came, then the use of a camera, or better still a video recorder can capture the feeling of those surroundings quite well. An illustration of a house where someone lived, the village, the local church, prominent buildings, local occupations, and for the more morbid amongst us, gravestones can enliven your family history when you prepare it for consumption by other interested parties.

### Family gatherings

If a family gathering is held, it can be quite enlightening to record members attending, especially if it is a large gathering covering a number of generations and involving quite distant cousins. Family characteristics can be noted in reviewing the tape, and shared characteristics between groups of family members can be linked with photographs and recollections of particular significant ancestors.

# CHAPTER FIVE

# *Branching out:*
# *Historical Sources back to 1841*

So far we have looked only at what could be described as basically 'genealogical sources', giving details of births, baptisms, marriages, deaths and burials. These record major events in individuals' lives and provide family links. They give us the basic facts from which we can construct a family tree. Of course these sources sometimes also give us a bit extra, such as the occupations and residences of our relatives, but for our purposes they are important for the genealogical information. If you want to build up a real family history, rather than just a genealogy, you will need to move on to researching in what we will describe as 'historical sources'. These record details of individuals' lives through *dates, places* and *activities* which are additional to the major 'life events' covered by the 'genealogical sources' and are very varied.

## 'The real thing': primary sources

Primary, or original, sources compiled at the period of time being studied are the basis of all research and fall into several categories, so firstly we will have a look at various listings, which tend to cover a wider range of the population than other sources.

## Listings

*Valuation Rolls, 1855-*

These rolls were compiled as lists of those liable to pay tax on the value of their property (rates) and are arranged by the address of the property concerned. From 1855 onwards there are annual rolls for each burgh and county, listing properties with the names and designations of the proprietor, tenant and occupier and its value. Unfortunately, occupiers of property at a rental of less than £4 a year did not have to be named and only the heads of households were named.

These records, a complete set of which are available in the Scottish Record Office, can be difficult to search, being arranged by address rather than by individuals' names. This means that if you are searching for a family in a large town, but do not have an address, you will probably have to hunt laboriously through several volumes which may be oddly arranged and whose arrangement may change from year to year. Sometimes the names of streets changed over a period of years and also the street numbers. Should you happen to be interested in Edinburgh or Glasgow, you will encounter extra problems, although there is a source of valuation records for Glasgow which may provide some consolation. The Valuation Rolls for these two cities are divided up by parishes, up to 1895 in Edinburgh and 1909 in Glasgow, and after these dates, by wards. In order to track down the street you are looking for, you could consult large-scale Ordnance Survey maps of the period, street directories, which show the ward numbers of streets, or, for Glasgow, the 1875-6 index of streets, giving the parishes for each street. After 1912, the Valuation Rolls for Edinburgh have street indexes. The Glasgow and Edinburgh street indexes are to be found in the Scottish Record Office.

Otherwise, those materials for tracking down a specific street relating to Edinburgh can be found in Edinburgh Central Library and those for Glasgow in the Mitchell Library there. Some Valuation Rolls can be found in local reference libraries or archives, but they usually only relate to the period after about 1880.

The other source for Glasgow mentioned above is the Valuation Roll Index, covering the Rolls for 1832, 1861, 1881 and 1911. Available in Glasgow City Archives, this computerised database arose out of a project on housing patterns in Glasgow from 1832 to 1911 conducted by the University of Strathclyde and contains the names of 352,486 individuals who were proprietors or occupiers in Glasgow during this period. Along with the names, it gives their occupations and addresses and is searched by names. A reference number is also given, but the Rolls themselves for this period are not held in the Glasgow City Archives.

There are also some earlier Valuation Rolls which are described in Chapter 6.

*Electoral Registers*

Also useful are the Electoral Registers, although they have not survived as well as the Valuation Rolls. Before the Reform Act of 1832 was passed, only a very small percentage of the population was entitled to vote, but from 1832 onwards, this percentage increased with the passing of several other Reform Acts. Details of who was allowed to vote can be found in *Electoral registers since 1832* by Jeremy Gibson and Colin Rogers. Very briefly, from 1832 to 1867 electors in parliamentary elections were male proprietors or tenants of lands or houses. In 1868 the category of male lodgers paying an annual rent of at least £10 was added. Women, although not receiving the vote in parliamentary elections until 1918, were given the vote in burgh council and county council elections from 1882 and 1889 respectively if they were proprietors or tenants. These women voters are recorded in separate registers for local government elections. Obviously, until 1918, there was a considerable proportion of the population who could still not vote, since from 1910 to 1918 the electorate in Scotland almost trebled. For most of the period, in the cities, the names are arranged by electoral wards. Despite this, you may still be able to pinpoint the address of relatives at a particular date, which could in turn help you to locate them in the Census returns. The information provided for the period 1832–1918 is the name, occupation, whether a proprietor, tenant or prosperous lodger and the property which qualified the elector to vote. It should be remembered that the elector may not be living at the address of the property which entitled him to vote.

The registers which have survived are scattered, some in the Scottish Record Office, particularly those between 1832 and the 1870s, and others in local archives and libraries. The Mitchell Library has a continuous set for Glasgow from 1846 appearing annually, except for periods during the two World Wars. There are separate registers for the burghs and counties. In many cases, a constituency consisted of several burghs perhaps in more than one county, while the registers for the counties are listed by parish. There are also some registers for the burghs among the Sheriff Court records and other odd registers in some Gifts and Deposits collections of the Scottish Record Office.

## Street and trade directories

Other listings which can prove very helpful are street and trade directories which are available mainly for the large cities. There are long runs of Post Office Directories for Edinburgh (annual from 1805) and Glasgow (annual from 1803), with a few other directories dating back to

1783 in Glasgow and 1773 in Edinburgh. Once again the coverage is quite limited, particularly in the early years, and tends to include the notable and well-off members of society, those with their own business or trade and those in official positions. Often these directories consist of three listings, one alphabetically by surname, one street by street and another for trades and businesses. Businessmen may be listed under both a business and home address or perhaps they may own several shops, each being mentioned individually. Although mainly useful for researching the cities, a few directories were published covering the Scottish counties, such as *Slater's Directory* and the *County Directory*, so you may be lucky enough to find some information there.

These directories can be found in large reference libraries or in local libraries in the area the directory covers.

To give an example of the kind of detail that these directories can contain, here is one from our own research:-

As a mail-coach guard, John McPhail merited inclusion in the Glasgow directories from 1801 to 1805:

M'Phail, J. Greenock mail-coach guard, Old Wynd.

Later in the century we can see the appearance of one of John's grandsons, first in the Directory for 1857–1858:

Dougall, John, tobacconist and tallow chandler,
15 1/2 Main Street, Calton; house, 17 Green Street, do.

From the next year, he was in business with his brother, and similar entries appear for several years and then stop. John later entered the medical profession and so pops up again in a new guise in the Directory for 1870–1871:

Dougall, John, physician and surgeon,
115 Paisley road; house, 119 do.

As you will see, he has two entries, one for his home

address and the other for that of his medical practice. He was also Medical Officer of Health for Kinning Park for a number of years, and since lists of such officials are included in some directories, he is also mentioned in that capacity in a section on the Burgh of Kinning Park.

You might also be able to use street directories to trace a private resident over a number of years, and if they have been listed regularly and are of a good age, their disappearance from the Directory can be a clue that they have died. Other sources can then be used to confirm this or otherwise. Two unmarried Holton sisters lived together in Uxbridge Road, London for many years in the early part of this century. By this date, a good number of private residents were being included in the street directories in addition to the notables, business and trades people and those in the professions. As a result, the Holton sisters could be traced year after year at the same address, until the death of Laura Elizabeth Holton in 1919. Another reason why a name which had been regularly included in a directory should then disappear could be a move out of the area, particularly if the person was not elderly.

## Church members

Quite a number of lists of church members from the nineteenth century are kept in the Scottish Record Office, some being separate lists (entitled list of communicants, communion roll or something similar) and others being included in kirk session minutes. Sometimes these give information about parishioners who had moved from another parish and the date they joined the church. It might also be worth checking whether the church had an account book listing those who rented seats in the church, a practice which was quite common at one time. These lists exist for both the Church of Scotland and other churches, and local archives also hold this type of material.

## Poor Law records

Although 1845 saw the passing of the Poor Law (Scotland) Act, this did not bring about a major change either in those entitled to help or in those running the system. Normally, only the poor who were over the age of 70, those unable to work due to disability or insanity, or children who had been orphaned or were destitute, were eligible for poor relief. The unemployed who were fit to work received no help for themselves, but their children might qualify. Basic responsibility for assisting the poor lay with the parish in which they were born or had lived for five years.

Parochial boards were set up after the 1845 Act to run the system, but in practice most of their members were the same people who had managed poor relief before 1845. As a result, the records often appear in kirk session records or heritors' records, kept in the Scottish Record Office. (The heritors were the principal landowners of the parish.) Where separate records exist for the parochial boards and their successors (from 1894), the parish councils, these are found among county council, district council and burgh records, stored mainly in local archives. A small number are kept in the Scottish Record Office.

The information provided in the poor relief records from 1845 is certainly better than for the earlier period, giving the age, place of birth and the name and age of the pauper's spouse and children whether they were living in the same residence or not.

There were applicants who were not successful and often they are mentioned in parochial board minutes, or in a separate list. Should they have made an appeal against the decision, their case would be recorded in the sheriff court records in the Scottish Record Office.

Particular to the Highlands and Islands were the destitution boards created in 1846 to provide money, meal or work for those affected by the failure of the potato crop. Their records cover the years 1847 to 1852 and are also in the Scottish Record Office.

Glasgow is fortunate in having a Poor Relief Applications database maintained in Glasgow City Archives. This covers the period from about 1850 to about 1900, with over 300,000 entries, and can be searched by personal names. It can be particularly useful in tracing birthplaces of many poor Irish who flooded into Glasgow in the middle of last century and is very easy to use. For example, a search for Margaret Conway, whose maiden surname was Gray, brings up this entry in the index:

| Name 2 | Name 1 | Name 3 | Born | Birthplace |
|--------|--------|--------|------|------------|
| Conway | Margaret | Gray | 1847 | Calton |

As you can see, married women are indexed under both their married and maiden surnames. A more detailed entry can now be called up on the computer screen, which gives us the additional information that the application for poor relief was made in 1880 and quotes a reference so that the original document can be requested. This lists the children's names and ages and the addresses at which the family lived over the preceding few years as well as some other information.

## Occupational records

### Coal miners

Being one of the main Scottish industries during the nineteenth century and the first half of the twentieth century, mining was a major employer, so there is a fair chance that one of your relatives may have been a miner.

The records in which you may trace some information are firstly, those of the National Coal Board. These records, kept in the Scottish Record Office, include the records of coal mining companies from before nationalisation in 1947 which date back in some cases to the eighteenth century. Most, however, are twentieth century and the details usually just consist of the names of miners with the work they had done and what they were paid.

At one time, many landowners ran mines on their estates and their records may be in the Gifts & Deposits collections in the Scottish Record Office.

### Railwaymen

Most of the surviving records of the many railway companies which used to exist in Scotland are kept in the Scottish Record Office. Some of the records of staff give the employee's date of birth and details of the various posts held while working for the company. The best collection of staff records is that of the North British Railway Company, and there are also some railway records in the Gifts & Deposits collections.

To utilise these sources you will need to have an idea which company your relative worked for. Helpful for this purpose is *British railways pre-grouping atlas and gazetteer* (published by I. Allan, 1976), which gives information about the companies before 1923.

For a more detailed survey of this subject, have a look at *Was your grandfather a railwayman?* edited by Tom Richards, 1995.

### Armed forces

Since the Army and Navy were run from London, almost all the records are held in the Public Record Office at Kew. For detailed information about the many manuscript sources which are held there you should check *Tracing your ancestors in the Public Record Office,* by Cox/Padfield.

Since these records are kept outside Scotland, you may

find it particularly useful to try tracing your relative in printed sources available in large reference libraries.

## Royal Navy

As far as the Navy is concerned, the printed sources include officers only, and so are of limited use. The annual *Navy list* and *The new Navy list*, 1839–1855, cover this period, but the *Naval biographical dictionary* by W. R. O'Byrne, published in 1849, gives more information for all the officers ranked lieutenant and above, who were active or retired in 1846. The father of the officer is often listed, making this a very useful source.

As already mentioned, there are many sources available in the Public Record Office, but as you can imagine, it is much easier to trace an officer than a rating. One of the main sources which lists all the officers and ratings on board a particular ship is the series of ships' musters held in the Public Record Office covering Scotland from 1707 to 1878. These give the place of birth and usually the age of ratings, but the big disadvantage is that you must know the name of the ship on which your relative served. Fortunately, from 1853, you can trace any naval seaman by name only, in the Continuous Service Engagement Books 1853–1872 and the Registers of Seamen's Services 1873–1895. Here you will find the date and place of birth and details of his service.

## Army

Once again, the main printed source, *The Army list*, first issued in 1740 and then annually from 1754, gives officers only and there are manuscript lists of officers for 1707–1752 in the Public Record Office at Kew. Most important amongst the manuscript sources for other ranks are the Muster Books and Pay Lists, the main series beginning in 1732. You will need to know the regiment your relative served in to use these records, but if you manage to trace him back to the date of enlistment, you should find his age and the place he enlisted, although not always his place of birth. Another useful series of records are the Soldiers' Documents 1760–1913, which give details of soldiers who were discharged to pension. These are arranged by regiment (to 1872), then in four categories (to 1883), and finally the arrangement is alphabetical by surname. The information given relates to the soldier's army service as well as his age, place of birth and previous occupation. After 1883, some additional details of family are listed. These sources are all housed in the Public Record Office.

There are some details of Militia amongst the Sheriff Court and County Council records and in some Gifts & Deposits collections in the Scottish Record Office, and also housed there are some Ministry of Defence records with lists of members of Territorial and Auxiliary Forces Associations. Information on Volunteer Forces can also be found in some of the Gifts & Deposits collections.

### Royal Air Force

Unfortunately records of those serving in the RAF and its predecessors, the Royal Flying Corps and Royal Naval Air Service, are not generally available, but application can be made by relatives to RAF Personnel Management.

### Merchant seamen

The main sources of information on merchant seamen in this period are agreements made between the masters of ships and crew members before they set sail. Such agreements became compulsory in 1835, and as a result there are various crew lists in the Scottish Record Office,

Glasgow City Archives, the Public Record Office, the National Maritime Museum in London and the Memorial University, Newfoundland. The agreements quote the name, age and place of birth of the crew members, but unless you know the name of the ship to search, or in some cases the port, you will be looking for a needle in a haystack, or perhaps a fish in the ocean.

## Businesses

Many records of businesses have now found their way into record offices, and in some cases these include records giving employees' names, especially wages books. To see what is available, you will need to check with the Scottish Record Office, the National Register of Archives (Scotland), Glasgow University Archives and local archives. Glasgow University has a special section devoted to business records with a particularly good collection of material for the West of Scotland, while the Scottish Brewing Archive, also held there, includes records of many companies from the Edinburgh area. One other source available in the Glasgow University Archives is a computer index of bankruptcies for the period from about 1745 to 1914. This index is also available in the Scottish Record Office, where the original records concerning bankruptcies are held.

If you are looking for information about either the Bank of Scotland or the Royal Bank of Scotland you should note that they both have their own archives.

## Clergymen

Information on clergymen from most of the main denominations can be found in printed sources, the most important being the *Fasti Ecclesiae Scoticanae*. This consists of several volumes detailing the ministers of the

Church of Scotland from 1560 onwards and gives biographical and family information about them.

The other publications are listed in the Further Reading and Sources list. You may wish to look for additional information by consulting the records of the churches themselves or contacting the offices of the relevant denomination.


### School teachers

Many books have been written about individual schools in Scotland and so you might find it worthwhile to begin any search for relatives who were school teachers by investigating whether anything has been written about the school or area which interests you. Very useful here are *A bibliography of Scottish education before 1872* and *A bibliography of Scottish education 1872–1972* both by James Craigie, and the *Scottish education bibliography 1970–1990 on CD-ROM*. These list both books and articles, and if there is any material on your school or area, the chances are it will be mentioned.

Moving on to manuscript sources, which are in the Scottish Record Office or local archives, we find a change in responsibility for schools occurring in 1872 when education became compulsory in Scotland, with the passing of the Education (Scotland) Act. Before this time, teachers in the burghs were appointed by the Burgh Council and are recorded in the Council Minutes. Outwith the Burghs, the normal procedure was for the heritors and minister of each parish to nominate a schoolmaster who was interviewed by the presbytery to establish his suitability. Appointments of parish schoolmasters were mentioned in the Heritors' Records with the confirmation by the presbytery in the presbytery Minute Books. Since the schoolmaster often became the Session Clerk, he may also be mentioned in the Kirk Session records.

The formation of the Free Church of Scotland in 1843 also resulted in the founding of Free Church schools whose teachers were appointed by the Deacons of the Church. The Deacons' Court minutes are the source which records these appointments.

The problem of the lack of schools in the Highlands and Islands attracted special attention from three sources: the Government, the Society in Scotland for Propagating Christian Knowledge (SSPCK), and a Mr. James Dick.

There are records of grants made by the Government to finance extra schools in these areas for the period 1840 to 1863, and these name the schoolmasters receiving them.

The SSPCK also set up schools in the Highlands and Islands, and the most useful sources for the schoolmasters in this period are the scheme ledgers which cover 1771–1890 and the abstract of school returns, 1827–1878.

Finally we turn to Mr. James Dick. In accordance with his Will, the Dick Bequest Trust was set up to provide assistance to schoolmasters in country parishes in the counties of Aberdeen, Banff and Moray. The Trust's records begin in 1832 and may prove useful if you had a teacher relative working in that area. These records are also in the Scottish Record Office.

The Educational Institute of Scotland was founded in 1847 as a professional association for teachers, and its records, which are deposited in the Scottish Record Office, give the names of its members.

In 1872 the responsibility for the provision of schools passed to school boards which mentioned the appointment of teachers and pupil-teachers in their minute books. These usually formed part of the county council records and may be kept in local archives or libraries, although a few are in the Scottish Record Office.

There are some other sources detailed in *Tracing your Scottish ancestors*, by Cecil Sinclair, but these tend to cover short periods or only a small number of schools.

*Doctors*

A considerable amount of information is available about doctors from published sources, namely *The Medical register*, published annually from 1859 and *The Medical directory*. *The Medical directory* appeared from 1845 onwards, but note that Scottish doctors are listed in the *Medical directory for Scotland*, 1852–1860, and then the *London and provincial medical directory*, 1861–1869. *The Medical directory* is also an annual and gives more details than *The Medical register*. There is often a brief summary of the individual's career, with qualifications, positions held and perhaps references to any published work they had produced. John Dougall's entry in *The Medical register* for 1876 is as follows:

| Date of Registration | Name | Residence | Qualification |
|---|---|---|---|
| 1869 May 25 | DOUGALL, John | 115 Paisley Road, Glasgow | M.B. 1869, Mast. Surg. 1869, M.D. 1871, Univ. Glasg. |

In *The Medical directory* for 1875 we find a much fuller entry:

DOUGALL, John, 2, Cecil-pl. Glasgow – M.D. Glasg. 1871, M.B. and C.M. 1869; (Univ. Glasg.); Sec. Glasg. Southern Med. Soc.; Mem. Gen. Counc. Univ. Glasg.; Mem. Counc. Geol. Soc. Glasg.; Mem. Nat. Hist. Soc., Chem. Sect. Philos. Soc., and Med. Chir. Soc. Glasg.; Mem. Brit. Assoc. for Adv. of Sci.; Med. Off. Health Kinning Park. Author, 'On the Relative Power of various Substances to prevent Generation of Animalculae, with special reference to the Germ Theory of Putrefaction,' Trans. Brit. Assoc. Adv. Sci. 1871-2. Contrib. 'Putrefiers and Antiseptics,' Glasg. Med. Journ. 1873; 'The Dissemination of Zymotic Diseases by Milk,' Ibid, 1873; 'Case of Ovarian Dropsy during Pregnancy,' Obst. Journ. Gt. Brit. 1874; various other Contribs. to Med. Journs.

This information can lead to other sources, particularly

the records of the University at which he studied, which we will look at shortly.

If you are trying to trace a doctor from before 1858, it may be worth contacting one or more of the three professional bodies concerned with the profession, the Royal College of Surgeons of Edinburgh, the Royal College of Physicians and Surgeons of Glasgow, or the Royal College of Physicians of Edinburgh. The first two of these bodies could license surgeons and doctors to practise and have records of licentiates dating back to 1770 and 1785 respectively. In the case of the Royal College of Physicians of Edinburgh, the procedure was different and their licentiates would all have studied at a university. It should be said that these lists of licentiates include little information and the university records could be a more fruitful source for those doctors and surgeons who studied there.

## *Other medical and related professions*

Registers of nurses from 1885 to 1930 are preserved in the Scottish Record Office, while dentists and chemists can be sought in published annual registers from 1879 and 1869 respectively.

Another avenue for tracing medical workers, particularly those associated with hospitals, is the records of health boards, many of which begin in the eighteenth century. Of course these also include a good deal of information about patients, but being un-indexed, they could prove very difficult to use for this purpose. Major collections are preserved for Dumfries and Galloway Health Board at Crichton Royal Hospital, Dumfries; for Grampian Health Board at Aberdeen Royal Infirmary; for Greater Glasgow Health Board at Glasgow University Archives; and for Lothian Health Board at Edinburgh University Library.

*Lawyers*

Once again, printed sources will probably be the first port of call in the search for relatives in the legal profession. If your relative was an advocate, which meant he could plead cases in the Court of Session, he should appear in *The Faculty of Advocates in Scotland 1532–1943* (Scottish Record Society, 1944). Here you will normally find the name of the advocate's father, the date of his own birth and death and details of any marriages. Solicitors, or as they are sometimes called, Writers, may be mentioned in *The register of the Society of Writers to the Signet* (Clark, Constable, 1983), although this is not comprehensive. Many Aberdeen solicitors are listed in the *History of the Society of Advocates in Aberdeen* (New Spalding Club, 1912).

The main annual published list of lawyers is the *Scottish law list* published for 1848–49, and then the *Index juridicus: the Scottish law list* from 1852 onwards.

There are various manuscript records in the Scottish Record Office, but you will probably not need to resort to them for this period. Details can be found in Sinclair's book, *Tracing your Scottish ancestors*.

## Educational sources

*School pupils*

A small number of schools have published lists of pupils and you may be able to trace these in local libraries. Many admission registers have survived and also school log books, recording the day-to-day events in the schools. These log books do mention names of pupils, but apart from this, they can provide some anecdotal background information for your family history. These school records tend to date from 1872, but some are earlier and you will normally find them in local archives. Otherwise, there are

Leaving Certificate registers from 1908 in the Scottish Record Office, listing all those presented for the Leaving Certificate; however, there is a 75 year closure period on these.

## University students

All of the four oldest Scottish universities have published information about their former students, some much more extensively than others.

Glasgow has published matriculation albums for 1728–1858 and the roll of graduates, 1727–1897. The first of these gives fuller information than the second, usually listing the name of the graduate's father and other biographical details.

St. Andrews matriculation roll, 1747–1897, and for Aberdeen, the Roll of alumni in Arts of University & King's College and the Fasti academiae Mariscallanae Aberdonensis, 1593–1860, although published, are little more than lists of names.

Finally, Edinburgh has only published lists of graduates in particular subjects.

Some other published lists are mentioned in the list of Further reading and sources.

It may be worthwhile contacting the University itself, which will probably have some unpublished records.

Now is the time to have a look at what the Glasgow University roll of graduates has to say about John Dougall. Under *Dougall, John* we find three entries. The first is obviously the one we are looking for, but the third, John M'Phail Dougall, was a son of the first John Dougall who also became a doctor. Here they both are:

Dougall, John,          M.B., C.M. 1869, M.D. 1871.
  Catrine; Glasgow (Lecturer on Clinical Medicine in
  Royal Infirmary; Professor of Materia Medica in St.
  Mungo's College).
Dougall, John M'Phail,     M.B., C.M. 1880, M.D. 1886.
  Glasgow; York; Glasgow; Dunoon; Welburn, Yorks.

As you can see, the various residences of the graduates are given.

An example from the Glasgow University matriculation albums illustrates the extra information you may find:

> 1834 A.D.
> 13232 RICARDUS SHAEN filius natu secundus Samuelis jurisconsulti in parochia de Hatfield Peverell et comitatu de Essex.
> Born in 1817. B.A. 1836 M.A. 1837. Minister at (1) Lancaster, 1842-45, (2) Edinburgh, 1845-50, (3) Dudley, 1852-55, (4) Royston, Herts., 1855-94. Died 24th January, 1894.

### Students of other educational institutions

A number of Scottish colleges were founded in the nineteenth century, and records of students have often survived. Jordanhill College of Education, now the Faculty of Education of the University of Strathclyde, has student registers from the middle of the nineteenth century, as well as various other sources such as letter books which often mention students.

You should contact the particular College itself to confirm whether any relevant documents have survived, and if so, where they are kept.

## Newspapers

Although these can be a very useful and illuminating source, particularly for filling in interesting details about individuals, they are often very difficult to use, given that most are un-indexed. This means some very laborious searching, especially for the most interesting news items. There are also the notices of births, marriages and deaths, and obituaries for well-known characters from the area, which are fairly easy to locate in each issue of the paper, but to pick up news stories, your task is much more difficult. *The Glasgow Herald* has an index for the period 1906–1984, and recently, a number of projects have been set up to index local newspapers, but the proportion covered is very small. To follow up this line of research, contact the local library for the area you are interested in and cross your fingers that an index has been produced.

To trace whether there are any newspapers covering the area and period you are interested in, consult the *Directory of Scottish newspapers* compiled by Joan P. S. Ferguson, which also lists where copies can be found.

## The 'real thing', once removed: secondary sources

### *Local histories and family histories*

Although the original, or primary, sources are the basis of all research, secondary sources such as local and family histories are worth consulting not only for the possibility of finding specific information about your family, but also to gather background historical information relating to a particular locality or family. Usually you will find a good collection of such works in the local library or in the main reference libraries such as Edinburgh Central Library or the Mitchell Library in Glasgow. To investigate whether any histories have been published about the area or family you are researching, consult, for local histories, *A contribution to the bibliography of Scottish topography* by Sir Arthur Mitchell and C. G. Cash, (Scottish History Society, 1917), *A bibliography of works relating to Scotland,1916–1950* by P. D. Hancock (Edinburgh University Press, 1959) and the *Bibliography of Scotland* produced by the National Library of Scotland, covering the period 1976 onwards; and for family histories, *Scottish family histories* compiled by Joan P. S. Ferguson.

*Biographical reference sources*

You might think it unlikely that any of your family would appear in dictionaries of biography, but since these are fairly accessible in reference libraries and also since as your research progresses, you may discover new family names and people of some importance, it is worth looking.

The main reference work of British biographies is the *Dictionary of National Biography*, or *DNB*. This massive work was published in 63 volumes, from 1885 onwards, with three supplementary volumes appearing in 1901. Since then, a new volume has been issued covering roughly each ten-year period, and then volumes for 1981–1985 and 1986–1990. It has recently been published on CD-ROM. This work contains biographies of individuals arranged alphabetically, but obviously many other names are briefly mentioned and in the CD-ROM version it is possible to search for these. As a result, the CD-ROM is a valuable asset.

A much more recent production is the *British biographical archive*, published by Saur on microfiche in two series. This includes entries from several hundred reference works published in the period 1601–1978, but not including the *DNB* or *Who was who*. It is only likely to be available in very large reference libraries.

The volumes of *Who was who* are compiled from '*Who's who*' and include many who have not gained an entry in the DNB. These cover from 1897 onwards.

Another work of possible use is *Modern English biography*, by Frederic Boase, first published in 1892–1921, which, despite its title, includes many Scots. This work, in six volumes, provides brief biographies of persons who died between 1851 and 1900.

Specifically Scottish biographies are covered by *A biographical dictionary of eminent Scotsmen* by Robert Chambers, published in 1835, and *The Scottish Nation* by

William Anderson, published in 1875, but only fairly major figures are included. *The Scottish Nation* includes information on surnames and families as well as on individuals. There is also the recent *Chambers Scottish biographical dictionary*, but again, this covers only the most famous.

If you think you have a connection with the nobility or landed gentry, you should consult *Burke's Peerage, Burke's Landed Gentry, Debrett's Peerage* and, in particular, for Scotland, *The Scots Peerage* by Sir James Balfour Paul. There are also a number of biographical dictionaries dealing with important figures associated with a particular area, such as Eyre-Todd's *Who's who in Glasgow in 1909*, or connected with a subject such as science or music, for example *British musical biography,* by Brown and Stratton published in 1897. Let us return to our old friend John Dougall and see whether he has an entry in *Who's who in Glasgow in 1909*. As it happens, he not only has an entry, including a photograph, but since he died in 1908 it is a very full entry covering his whole career. His year of birth is given and some details about his early life, including a mention of his father and his mother's uncle 'Sir' Duncan McArthur. As mentioned in Chapter 1, Duncan was never actually knighted and some of the other information about him is inaccurate, but it was based on fact. The entry continues with mention of John's career in the soap and candle-making business and his eventual entry into the medical profession, in which he acted as a dresser to Joseph Lister in Glasgow Royal Infirmary and received notable appointments as Medical Officer of Health for Kinning Park and Professor at the St. Mungo College. A good deal of the information mentioned here had already come to light from other sources such as street directories, university records and medical directories, but to discover a biographical notice usually adds a few personal details about the individual which may be impossible to find otherwise. For example, we are told that John acted as a precentor in various churches and also that as a young man he narrowly escaped death when working in Tennant's Works at St. Rollox. He rushed into a cloud of chlorine gas at a new bleaching-powder chamber and almost suffocated.

This entry was a great find, and if you think a relative of yours might be included in a similar type of publication, it is well worth checking. The local library or a large reference library may be able to help you here.

# CHAPTER SIX

# Digging Deeper: Sources before 1841

## Old Parish Registers

As you move back in time in the search for your family roots, you will reach the period before Civil Registration (1855) and the earliest useful Census (1841). The most important source for you now will be the Old Parish Registers (OPRs). These are the registers of baptisms or births, marriages or the proclamations of banns and burials or deaths, kept in each Church of Scotland parish, of which there are about 900. There is no standard date when these began and their starting date as well as the way in which they were kept was very much dependent on each individual parish minister. The earliest Parish Registers in Scotland begin in 1553, but only a few date back to the sixteenth century and many began in the eighteenth century. There are some which commenced only in the early nineteenth century and even a few places without any Parish Registers. Many lack burial or death registers. In theory, all the registrations should have been made in the Parish Registers, but in practice, they are far from complete. Those who were members of other churches, such as the Roman Catholic Church, may not have registered these events in the Church of Scotland registers. Perhaps they will be recorded in registers kept by their own church (see **Nonconformist records** later in this chapter) or not recorded at all. It is always best to consult the OPRs first, however, since many nonconformists will be registered there, plus the fact that they are much more easily accessible and searchable.

Another factor affecting the completeness of these Registers was the huge growth of population in the towns from the end of the eighteenth century. With the movement of population, people's ties with the Church could become tenuous and it was not so likely that registrations would be made. In addition, from 1783 to 1794 a stamp-duty of threepence was payable by anyone registering an event in the Parish Registers. This seriously affected the number of registrations made.

John McPhail and Florence McArthur were married in 1787 at Glasgow High Church, but Florence's baptism does not seem to have been recorded, although her brother Duncan's baptism appears in 1773. We know from his Will that he had several other brothers and sisters, but only some have been traced in the OPRs.

When considering the amount of information found in the Parish Registers, the first thing to say is that there is normally a good deal less than you would have found in the Civil Registers. Baptisms are likely to give the name and date of baptism of the child, his parents' names, their place of residence and possibly the father's occupation. Marriage entries usually refer to the proclamation of marriage which was made in the parishes of both the bride and groom. It is possible that more information may be given in one Parish Register than the other, and sometimes there is a statement that the marriage did actually take place, with the date. In most cases, the names of the bride and groom, their residences and the date of proclamation are given. Burials will often mention little more than the name of the deceased and the date of burial.

Although this is the information which you might

expect to find, it is possible that, in a parish with an interested and conscientious minister, various other details may be included. Quite often the mother's maiden name is given in baptismal entries, and godparents' names could be mentioned. Since these were very often relatives, this could be useful. The actual date of birth might also be given. Additional information found in marriage registers could be parents' names and the occupation of the groom, but almost certainly not ages, which is a great pity from the genealogist's point of view. Burials might give the age of the individual, the cause and date of death and parents' names in the case of a young child. If the deceased still had a spouse living, then his or her name could be included and if they were either a widow or widower, again this might be specified.

Given the comparative lack of information included in the OPRs, one of the major difficulties encountered is the problem of identifying the person you are looking for. Common names, particularly in the towns and Highland parishes, and the frequent use of the same few Christian names in the same family, can make it very difficult to decide who is who, if there is no additional evidence, such as ages or occupations. All you can do in such cases is gather all the information available from every possible source to assist you in making a positive identification.

The searching of the OPRs has been made much easier by the provision of various indexes, including the IGI, which has already been described in Chapter 3. You must remember that the IGI does not include burials and deaths. The original Parish Registers are kept in New Register House and there you will find computerised indexes to the baptisms and marriages, but only a small number of paper indexes to burials. The computer index can be searched for the whole of Scotland or by a particular county, and there is also a microfiche version available in Family History Libraries of the Mormon Church and in some public libraries.

Having found a reference in the indexes which seems relevant, you will then need to look at the full entry and you will be given a microfilm copy, since the originals are not normally used nowadays because of the problems of wear and tear. It is disappointing not to be able to consult these documents from the time of your ancestors, but as genealogy is so popular now, the necessity of preservation has to come first.

## Monumental inscriptions

As a supplement to the records of burials in the Old Parish Registers, it is well worth searching for monumental inscriptions. The information recorded on gravestones is often fuller than in a burial entry, giving the date of death rather than burial and possibly a mention of the occupation and residence of the person. Probably the biggest advantage, however, of finding an inscription from a gravestone, is the likelihood that other members of the family will be mentioned. This opens up the possibilities of discovering previously unknown relatives, such as other children or parents of the deceased. Quite often the burial plot, or lair, was used by the family for several generations, so stones which pre-date the introduction of Civil registration in 1855 can be particularly helpful in establishing family links which are difficult or even impossible to discover in the less reliable church registers.

To find this sort of information, you may want to wander round a peaceful country churchyard in search of your family's gravestones, but in many cases this will not be the most effective means of finding the desired details. The weather has taken its toll of many stones which have become indecipherable, but, fortunately, a great deal of effort by various enthusiasts has resulted in the transcribing of very many monumental inscriptions. This work has been co-ordinated mainly by the Scottish Genealogy Society and copies are available in the Society's Library in Edinburgh, and in the Scottish Record Office. Local libraries should also have copies of the volumes covering their own locality.

Although their significance is greater before 1855, inscriptions have continued up until the present day and so should not be ignored as a possible source for the more recent period. Since the work of transcription has concentrated on the pre-1855 stones, it may prove more difficult to trace later inscriptions. Check local libraries and archives for lists. In the cities, there are many cemeteries run by the Parks Departments of the local authorities. Although they do not record the inscriptions, lists of interments have usually survived, kept either by the Parks Department or deposited in a local archives office. If you manage to track down an entry in one of these lists, it will probably give a location for the burial, where you can then look for a gravestone and maybe find a mine of information. On the other hand, on arriving at the spot, you could discover that no stone was erected. It is just one of those chances you take in the family history search.

## Wills and Testaments

In Scotland in former times, unlike England, only moveable property such as money, furniture and equipment connected with a trade, could be bequeathed in a will. As a result, land or houses could not be included and this remained the situation until after 1868. For records of the inheritance of land or houses, see the next section.

On the death of an individual, in theory, someone should be appointed to administer the disposal of any moveable property and that person is named the executor. In cases where the individual left a will, an executor was usually named in it, but if there was no will, the deceased is 'intestate' and an executor was appointed by the appropriate court. Both situations required the confirmation of the executor by the court, which is how the transaction came to be legally recorded. The resulting records are called Testaments, either a testament-testamentar if there is a will, or a testament-dative if there is not.

It is unfortunately the case that very few people left wills, and even those who did may not have had an executor confirmed, but if you are lucky enough to trace some wills relating to your family, you should find them good sources of genealogical and historical information.

The information usually found in testaments is the name and residence of the deceased, date of death, confirmation of the executor, inventory of moveable property and a will if there is one. Supposing there is a will, you might find quite a number of relatives mentioned, but particularly children of the individual. This could prove some genealogical links and perhaps mention some children who do not appear in the Parish Registers. From the historical point of view, a good deal of social and economic history can be revealed, giving an idea of the social standing of your relative. You should beware, though, since because the eldest son inherited all of the land and buildings and did not receive any of the moveable property if his father died without a will, he may not be mentioned in the testament. Wills are the most likely source of details of your family's day-to-day life and therefore a very valuable source.

All Scottish Testaments are stored in the Scottish Record Office except for those from Orkney and Shetland, which are kept in the local archives. As with many of these types of records, the means of searching them are many and varied. Before the Reformation, control over testaments was held by Church courts, but these were abolished and in 1564 Commissary Courts were established. There were eventually 22 of these and one of their functions was to confirm testaments, with the Edinburgh Commissariot having authority throughout Scotland and for those who died abroad. This means you need to check the Edinburgh Court as well as the local court for the area in which your relative died.

In 1823 the Sheriff Courts took over responsibility for testamentary matters.

There are various indexes available including one for each Commissariot to 1800 published by the Scottish Record Society. From 1876–1959 there are annual print-ed volumes for the whole of Scotland available in the Scottish Record Office, but for the various assorted indexes for the intervening period see *Tracing your Scottish ancestors* by Sinclair.


## Retours, or Services of Heirs

As we mentioned in the previous section, land or houses, or 'heritable property' as it is described, could not be left in a will until after 1868. Inheritance of this type of prop-erty was recorded in the Retours, or Services of Heirs, either special retours, which named the property, or gen-eral retours, which did not. The other details to be found are the names of the heir and the relative whose property is being inherited, their relationship and possibly the date of death of the relative.

The retours begin in 1530 and were written in Latin until 1847, except for the years 1652–1659. It is worth searching for a period after the death of the earlier prop-erty owner because the retours were sometimes not recorded until well after the date of death. Although the originals are in the Scottish Record Office, there are printed indexes which can be found in large reference libraries and these can sometimes provide sufficient detail, especially in a case when a son succeeded his father. The indexes have the added advantage of being in English. The index to 1700 is arranged by county and gives references to two published volumes of summaries of the retours, which include most of the information. These summaries are also available in large reference libraries. From 1700 to 1859, each volume of the *Indexes to the Services of Heirs in Scotland* covers ten years, and then they become annual.

## Sasines

One of the most important series of records held in the Scottish Record Office are the Registers of Sasines, which record the transfer of ownership of land and houses from 1617. This is a wonderful resource and there is no equivalent in England. If your family owned even a small piece of land or a small cottage, it should be possible to gather some details about them from the Sasines. Quite often fathers granted land to their children and there could be a mention of previous grants with the chance of other relatives being named. Even if no family links are established in the transfer of the property concerned, there will be information about its location and size (if land) and often the occupations of the two parties involved.

From 1617 to 1868 there was a General Register of Sasines, recording property in any area of Scotland, and various Particular Registers of Sasines recording property in a particular county. The period 1869 onwards is covered by a Register for each county. As well as these, the Royal Burghs had their own registers, beginning at various dates. To make a comprehensive search for the earlier period you will need to check three registers if you think your family had property in a Royal Burgh; firstly the Burgh Register, secondly the Particular Register of Sasines for the area concerned, and finally the General

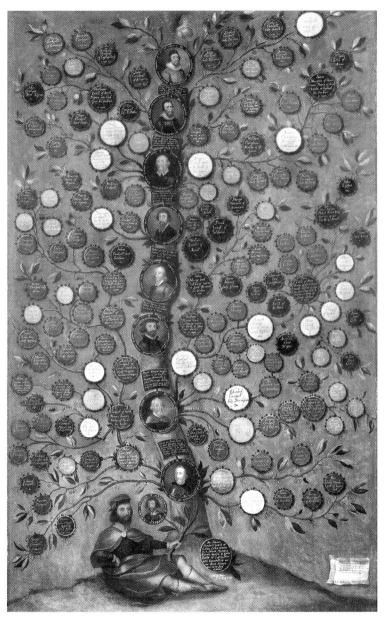

A decorative family tree. The Campbells of Glenorchy, by George Jamesone, 1635. *Scottish National Portrait Gallery.*

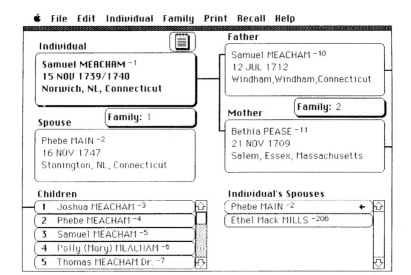

Pedigree search screen from the Personal Ancestral File (PAF), a genealogical software package.

General Register House, the main site of the Scottish Record Office.
*By permission of the Keeper of the Records of Scotland.*

Left: Historical Search Room, Scottish Record Office.
*By permission of the Keeper of the Records of Scotland.*

Below: West Register House, home of the National Register of Archives (Scotland).
*By permission of the Keeper of the Records of Scotland.*

## The UK and Ireland

The information in these pages is intended as a "virtual reference library" in support of the general discussions and Usenet newsgroup soc.genealogy.uk+ireland (and its mailing list equivalent, which can be joined by sending the message SUBSCRIBE GENUKI-L to listserv@mail.eworld.com).

The **UK and Ireland** are regarded, for the purposes of this Genealogical Information Service, as being made up of **England**, **Ireland** (i.e. *Northern Ireland* and the *Republic of Ireland*), **Wales**, and **Scotland**, together with the **Channel Islands** and the **Isle of Man**. Together, these constitute the *British Isles* - which is a geographical term for a group of islands lying off the north-west coast of mainland Europe. (Legally, the Channel Islands and the Isle of Man are largely self governing, and are not part of the United Kingdom.)

This page provides pointers to these six areas, plus information which relates to the UK and Ireland as a whole. The UK and Ireland is in fact divided into a large number of Administrative Regions, whose names are often abbreviated by genealogists using a set of three-letter "Chapman codes".

These codes are also given in a map showing the counties in England, Scotland and Wales prior to the re-organisation which took place in 1974 (1975 for Scotland). Riley Williams (u05rhw@abdn.ac.uk) prepared it originally, with modifications by Mike Fisher. The corresponding one for Ireland has been produced by Brian Randell based on a map obtained from Paddy Waldron.

### REGIONS

- England
- Ireland
- Scotland
- Wales
- Channel Islands
- Isle of Man

### INFORMATION RELATED TO ALL THE BRITISH ISLES

- Archives and Libraries
- Bibliography
- Chronology
- Church Records
- Description and Travel
- Emigration and Immigration
- Gazetteers
- Genealogy
- Handwriting
- Heraldry
- History
- Land and Property
- Maps
- Merchant Marine
- Military History
- Military Records
- Names, Personal
- Occupations
- Periodicals
- Probate
- Societies
- Taxation

#### Archives and Libraries:

There are a number of major national archives and libraries, which between them contain a vast amount of genealogical information - see:

- Public Record Office. For online copies of the PRO information leaflets see the genuki/PRO pages. The PRO also have a special Genealogists' page. Note: most Scottish records are held in the Scottish Record Office in Edinburgh.
- The Royal Commission on Historical Manuscripts,
- Society of Genealogists,
- Institute of Heraldic and Genealogical Studies,

One of the 'Genuki' pages on the World Wide Web.

Register. If their property was outwith the Royal Burghs, the second and third of these will have to be consulted.

Although there are some indexes, not all areas and periods have been covered. Here is a brief summary of the indexes available:

| | |
|---|---|
| General Register | 1617–1720 and 1781–1868 |
| Particular Registers | 1617–1780 some indexes, some of which have been published and 1781–1868 |
| Registers for each county | 1869– |
| Burgh Registers | some indexed from 1809 |

The index from 1781 is arranged by counties and covers both the General and Particular Registers, so this makes a search a little easier. It refers to the Sasine Abridgements which will probably give you all the information you require, but if you need to consult the full entries, they are often in Latin. It is helpful to be familiar with the layout if you are likely to be looking at the full entries and Gouldesbrough's *Formulary of old Scots legal documents* will give you guidance here. Both persons and places are indexed for 1781–1830 and 1872 onwards, but otherwise normally just the persons are indexed. The indexes of places for large towns in some cases list specific streets, but there are also entries such as *Glasgow: Tenements in*.

The vast majority of the Sasines are kept in the Scottish Record Office, but some Burgh Registers are in local archives, such as the Register for Glasgow which is in Glasgow City Archives. The Registers of Scotland, the organisation which now deals with the registration of land ownership, is based at Meadowbank House in Edinburgh, but there is also an office in Cowglen, Glasgow which stores the Sasine Abridgements for the 'counties' of Dunbarton, Glasgow and Renfrew. This may prove more convenient in some cases for researchers in the West of Scotland, but the drawback is that a charge is made for each person or property searched for.

The following is an example of an entry in the Sasine Abridgements for Fife :-

(1125)     May 10. 1785.
DAVID DRYSDALE, Smith, Freuchie, and Jean Peattie, his spouse, Seised, in fee & liferent respectively, Apr. 28. 1785, – in a Tenement in FREUCHIE, par. Falkland; – on Disp. by John Ramsay, Weaver, North Shields, to James Dryburgh, Merchant, Markinch, Dec. 31, 1773; and Disp. & Assig. by him, Nov. 6. 1784.        P. R. 35. 205.

## Registers of Deeds

These registers cover a wide variety of matters which involved some form of legal transaction. The most commonly recorded documents are bonds detailing loans of money while other Deeds deal with settlements of testaments, marriage contracts, arrangements for apprenticeships and miscellaneous agreements between individuals. Finding a Deed should fill in a little more detail of the life of the relative concerned and add some more colour to the picture you are building up.

Until 1809, deeds could be registered in any court, but from then on this function was restricted to the Court of Session, Sheriff Courts and Royal Burgh Courts. As in the case of retours, deeds are sometimes not registered until years after the transaction had taken place.

Here is a table giving brief details of the various courts, the dates of the registers and whether they are indexed:

| Name of Court | Registers | Indexes |
|---|---|---|
| Court of Session | from early sixteenth century | up to 1660: indexes covering short periods 1661–1707: complete indexes 1708–1769. indexes covering |

| | | short periods 1770 onwards: annual indexes (granters of deeds only) |
|---|---|---|
| Sheriff Courts | some from sixteenth century some published | very few |
| Royal Burgh Courts | some from sixteenth century | very few |
| Commissary Courts | up to 1808 | none |
| Local Courts | up to 1747 | none |

To make a thorough search, you will need to check the Court of Session Registers and the registers for any other court covering the area you are interested in. Most of these are in the Scottish Record Office but there may be some in local archives. It is also worth mentioning that there are many deeds in the Gifts and Deposits Collections in the Scottish Record Office, but it may be rather difficult to trace a relevant deed, although see Chapter 8.

## Kirk Session records

These consist of the records of the body which ran the business of each Church of Scotland parish and since in the past this covered most aspects of people's lives, a great variety of information can be found there. The major items which usually appear are the organisation of relief for the poor of the parish and the disciplining of wrong-doers, with the individual's names being listed. Misconduct of parishioners might be 'breaking the Sabbath,' by, perhaps, creating a disturbance when they should have been in Church, or – the most commonly mentioned offence – fornication. Other matters could include lists of communicants or church members and details of the appointment of schoolmasters. These records are a major source for information on the ordinary people, containing the main listings of the poor to be found, but since they are not indexed, it can be a laborious task to search them. The Scottish Record Office has a fairly complete collection of Kirk Session records but local archives also often have copies.

## Poor relief to 1845

Up until the Poor Law Act of 1845, assistance to the poor was organised by the heritors (principal landowners) and the Kirk Session of every parish. Sometimes separate lists were kept of payments to the poor of the parish, but more likely this information will be found mixed up with other business in the general records of the heritors and Kirk Sessions. Again the main collection of these is held in the Scottish Record Office with separate listings of heritors' records and church records which include those of the Kirk Sessions. In the burghs, although poor relief was dispensed, the records often give few details, but those for Edinburgh and Glasgow are rather more useful and can be found in the relevant local archive.

## Nonconformist records

Although in the past the vast majority of Scots were adherents of the Church of Scotland, there were many nonconformist churches whose records have survived in varying degrees of completeness and which tend to be scattered in various locations. From the eighteenth century up until the Disruption in 1843, there were various breakaways from the established Church of Scotland, with the Disruption, which resulted in the formation of the Free Church of Scotland, being the most important. After this, mergers of denominations began to take place and by 1929 many of these churches had reunited with the Church of Scotland. Many of the records of these churches are kept in the Scottish Record Office and include baptisms, marriages and burials, lists of communicants and minute books. Two of the main churches represented are the Free Church of Scotland and the United Presbyterian Church of Scotland.

The original records of the Roman Catholic Church, unlike those of the Church of Scotland, have not been gathered centrally, but the Scottish Record Office does have photocopies of many pre-1855 registers of baptisms, marriages and deaths, which could ease the searcher's task considerably. One register dates back to 1703, but in general they begin in the nineteenth century. The parish priests hold either the originals or copies of their own registers, while the Archives of the Archdiocese of Glasgow also have registers for some of the parishes in Glasgow and the surrounding area.

Again, in the case of the Episcopal Church of Scotland, most of the records are still held by the local clergy, with a few originals and microfilm copies in the Scottish Record Office. You should find the surveys of the National Register of Archives (Scotland) helpful here, since all known Episcopal Church records have been surveyed and lists produced. For more information about the National Register of Archives (Scotland) see page 79.

Finally, there are the Baptist, Congregational, Methodist, Quaker and Unitarian Churches. Some of their records are stored in the Scottish Record Office, and Glasgow City Archives have a sizeable collection of nonconformist records for almost all of these churches apart from the Roman Catholic Church. As you would expect, these cover Glasgow and surrounding areas, but the Congregational Church records come from all parts of Scotland. For the Baptist Church, the individual church should be contacted, and for nonconformist records in general it is worth checking the National Register of Archives (Scotland) for possible locations, or the headquarters of the Church concerned.

## Valuation Rolls before 1855

Some rolls exist in the Scottish Record Office for this earlier period, but they are isolated and sometimes they list the value of the lands but not the names of the proprietors and occupiers. The earliest of these date from 1643, while some have been published. You may find useful *A directory of land ownership in Scotland c. 1770* by Loretta R. Timperley, which takes its information mainly from Valuation Rolls. The early nineteenth century is better provided for, but, as in the case of the earlier period, in the Royal Burghs the tax was usually paid in one lump sum and those paying were not normally listed.

If you do find family members mentioned in Valuation Rolls, you will probably only succeed in locating them at a particular place at a particular date since the information will be very brief and is more likely to mention proprietors than occupiers. This information might, however, provide a basis for tracing them in the Registers of Sasines which would give much fuller details.

For more detailed information on what is available for Valuation Rolls in the Scottish Record Office, consult Sinclair's book.

## Hearth Tax and Poll Tax

These two taxes were introduced for fairly short periods in the 1690s, the Hearth Tax from 1691 to 1695 and the Poll Tax from 1693 to 1699, and although this is a fairly serious limitation, they do provide listings of a considerable proportion of the population. All landowners and tenants were liable to pay for the number of hearths in their houses, while the Poll Tax was levied on all adults who did not depend on charity. Unfortunately the records are not complete, and in the case of the Hearth Tax, some list the amount collected but not individual names. The arrangement of the records is by county and then by parishes, with the Poll Tax having two series of records which both need to be checked. If you do find your family mentioned in the Poll Tax records, children's names may also be included.

The original documents are in the Scottish Record Office, but there are some published lists.

## Trades

As you can imagine, those involved in trade tended to be concentrated in the Royal Burghs, where matters were well regulated. In order to be allowed to practise a trade in the Royal Burghs, an individual was required to be admitted as a burgess. Some lists of burgesses have been published by the Scottish Record Society, in particular those for Edinburgh (1406–1841) and Glasgow (1573–1846). Otherwise, admissions can be found in burgh records, some in the Scottish Record Office, but many in local archives. Since newly admitted burgesses were often sons or sons-in-law of burgesses, this relationship is mentioned in the records.

There also existed, in the burghs, influential craft guilds or incorporations which kept records of members, and here again they were often sons or sons-in-law of members or were apprenticed to a member of the craft. Published lists exist in some cases and the original records can be found in local archives, the Scottish Record Office or listed in the National Register of Archives (Scotland) surveys.

Because of the large proportion of burgesses and craft members who were admitted by right of their relationship to an existing member, it is possible to trace back several generations through these records, which can thus prove a very fruitful source.

For example, John Brock was admitted as a Glasgow Burgess in 1787 as eldest son of William Brock, weaver.

Checking back, we find that William had been admitted in 1776 as the eldest son of another William Brock, weaver. This William, the grandfather of John, appears in 1743 and was the eldest son of Robert Brock, deceased, gardener, who was admitted in 1719 as married to Agnes, daughter of the deceased John Duncan, gardener. We could then continue our search by following up the Duncan family. You can see the usefulness of this source, which, in this example, took us back four generations in only a few minutes of research.

The apprenticeship system was widespread until relatively recently and normally the father of the new apprentice entered into an agreement, called an indenture, with the master to whom his son was apprenticed. These are mentioned in the records of the craft concerned, but not many of the indentures themselves have survived.

Unfortunately, if your relatives were tradesmen beyond the burghs, there are unlikely to be any records available. The only sources for them are few and far between, being the records of mutual benefit societies such as the Society of Free Fishermen of Newhaven. The main repository for these is the Scottish Record Office.

Anyone selling alcoholic drink had, from 1756, to be licensed and this covered the burghs and the counties. The granting of these licences was carried out by the burgh court or the Justices of the Peace for the county, and their records are kept in the Scottish Record Office or local archives, beginning mainly in the nineteenth century.

### Merchant seamen

Although difficult to find without fairly precise details of the ship or port concerned, there are vouchers of payments of bounties for whaling (1750–1825) and for herring fishing (1752–1796). These vouchers named the crews and are available in the Scottish Record Office.

## Gifts and Deposits collections

This title covers a very wide range of documents which
have been gifted or lent to the Scottish Record Office by
individuals, families, businesses and organisations, and they
may provide you with useful information, particularly if
your family lived on a large estate. If the estate papers are
amongst the Gifts and Deposits collections, your family's
name may well be mentioned. Catalogues of the collections are available in the Scottish Record Office, but a
much more flexible finding aid is being developed in the
form of a computerised Gifts and Deposits Textbase. This
allows the searcher to look for any word or name which
appears in the entry for each document in a collection. The
entries include a brief description of the contents of the
document, and so names can often be mentioned, especially in the case of correspondence. A useful category of
material found in the Gifts and Deposits collections are
wages books and these can be much more easily traced on
the Textbase. A considerable percentage of the collections
is included on the Textbase, and it is growing all the time.

## National Register of Archives (Scotland)

You will have gathered by now that once you move
beyond the three main categories of records held in New
Register House, the Civil Registers, Census Records and
Old Parish Registers, most archival material is scattered in
various locations. Although there is never likely to be a
complete listing of all collections and their whereabouts,
the National Register of Archives (Scotland), or NRA(S),
is an attempt to provide one. Since its foundation in
1946, it has gathered information on and conducted surveys of archive collections held outwith the Scottish
Record Office by individuals, businesses and organisations, including local authority archives. Their lists of sur-

veys range from the very small to the very large. For example from the one page survey of the records of The Royal High School Athletic Club, Edinburgh Rugby Section to the 144 page survey of the Scottish Episcopal Church Congregations in the Diocese of Edinburgh, or large estate collections such as those of the Dukes of Hamilton, Argyll and Roxburghe.

The NRA(S) is administered by the Scottish Record Office based in its West Register House site in Charlotte Square, Edinburgh and the index to the surveys can be consulted in the Scottish Record Office, National Library of Scotland, many of the older university libraries and local authority archives. A computerised Textbase of these surveys is currently being developed by the Scottish Record Office. Any types of records can be listed and so if you have been unsuccessful in tracing a particular source in the obvious locations, it is worthwhile checking the NRA(S). For a possible way of searching this through the Internet, see Chapter 8.

### Making use of the sources

So these are the sources, or at least the main ones, but how can you make use of what you find? The historical information giving details about the lives of your family and the environment in which they lived can be very interesting, but we would hope that you will incorporate it into some form of narrative family history. We will describe some means of going about this in the next chapter. Before moving on to this stage, we should consider how to extend the framework of your family tree using the genealogical information you have gleaned from the sources described in this chapter and the preceding one.

The most important facts needed to make genealogical links are: name, date and place of birth or baptism, marriage and death or burial. If these are known, you will have a good chance of tracing a record of the event. This in turn may either make a genealogical link, with the parents' names given in a baptismal record or perhaps a father's name in a marriage entry, or give enough data to lead you back to an earlier event which can then establish a link. A record of burial giving the person's age may in some cases help you find the baptism, although you will probably need extra evidence to confirm this.

When tracing your family in the earlier period we have been looking at, you will very often find that only one of these important facts is known, this being the name. Everything else has to be sought out by deduction and by building up a body of evidence, similar to that in a legal case, in order to prove that each record that you find really does refer to the individual you are tracing and not to someone else of the same name.

In the case of working back from a marriage to a baptism, you will usually need to estimate the age of the bride and groom, since it is unlikely to be given. Then you can search for baptisms in the period calculated according to their estimated ages. This could range from 16 to perhaps 40, but is probably on average likely to be between 20 and 25, although average age at marriage has varied at different times in history and can also be affected by local conditions. You may have found one or both of the fathers' names in the marriage entry, which will be a big help in correctly identifying the baptism you are seeking.

The other factor, place, could also prove to be a problem. The marriage entry might state the parishes of the bride and groom, but if it does not, it is probable that the marriage took place in the bride's parish. All you can do, without evidence to the contrary, is deduce that the parish listed for each at their marriage was the one in which they were baptised. This, of course, may not be the case, and when no parishes are named, the task becomes more difficult, especially in the case of the groom.

In making the connection between a baptism and the marriage of the parents, things may be a little easier. The registers can be searched for possible older brothers and sisters and then the marriage, but you may find neither these nor a marriage, since the family could have moved from another parish where the marriage and other baptisms were registered. Another possibility, if baptisms are found but no marriage, is that the parish that you are searching in was the husband's parish but the marriage took place in the wife's parish.

Although in the past, movement was less common than today, especially over long distances, there was often movement in and out of parishes within a ten-mile radius, so if you lose trace of a family, you could try the few surrounding parishes.

One other consideration which may assist you is the traditional naming pattern often followed in Scotland. The eldest son was named after the father's father, the second son after the mother's father and the third son after the father. Daughters were named after first the mother's mother, then the father's mother and thirdly the mother. This can be used as a basis to work from, but should not be relied upon and would need confirmation from another source.

We have outlined here some of the difficulties you may encounter. You must be satisfied that you have made correct identifications for all those included in your family history. This is an area particularly studied by historical demographers in their work on nominal record linkage and its use in family reconstitution. If you want to follow up this important method of establishing reliable genealogical links, you should consult *Identifying people in the past,* by E. A. Wrigley (1973). Genealogists have always been used to making such links, but the historical demographers, looking at large numbers of families and making use of computers in their work, have formalised the methods. It is obviously important to make the correct links, and we hope that this section has emphasised this and given you some clues as to how to tackle this aspect of family history.

CHAPTER SEVEN

# *Writing it up*

As a hunter-gatherer in the field of family history you will probably amass quite a quantity of facts. Names, dates, occupations and other snippets of information will abound, but if you have followed our advice earlier in the book, these details should be well organised and easily accessible. What will almost certainly be lacking in your collection of family history materials is narrative. Perhaps you may have stories or reminiscences gathered from elderly relatives and written down or recorded on audio cassette. The collection could also include obituaries or newspaper reports about members of your family. However, this sort of material is not likely to occur often and, when it does, forms an isolated example of narrative. This chapter is about producing some form of continuous narrative history of your family in which you put flesh on the bones of the skeleton family tree you have constructed. In doing this, you will be able to bring together the fruits of your labours and present them in a readable form which, we hope, will prove to be not only a source of satisfaction to yourself, but also of interest to relatives and perhaps even a wider audience.

## When should this be done?

Obviously a reasonable amount of information is required

before making a start, but to put off too long is not advisable. You may have relatives who have helped you out with facts which they can remember and documents which they own and who are keen to see the results of your investigations. It is probably unlikely that you will complete your researches for a considerable time, if ever, so do not wait for that moment, particularly considering the fact that word-processing facilities are now widely available. This makes it very easy for you to begin constructing your narrative history in the knowledge that if you discover new information, it can easily be incorporated and printed out without the need for retyping whole sections or pages. Our advice would be to compose a basic narrative as soon as possible and update it regularly. When you decide it is full enough and in a presentable form, it can be printed out and reproduced for wider circulation.

## What form should it take?

The simplest form of written history which you might consider using is a family tree in chart form along with associated notes on the various individuals. The names on the chart, or charts, are numbered, and then, on separate pages, fuller details can be given for each numbered individual. These notes could range from the dates and places of birth, baptism, marriage, death and burial to extensive biographies, depending on the information you have and what you feel is appropriate.

We will now look at writing a narrative family history which may use family tree charts to increase the clarity, but with the narrative as the basis rather than in the previous format described, where the chart is the basis.

The first main type is that found in *Burke's Peerage* and *Burke's Landed Gentry*, which uses indentation on the page, along with various sequences of numbers and letters, to indicate different generations. The information about each individual tends to be relatively brief in this form of history.

If you are interested in using this format, have a look at some examples in Burke's publications mentioned above, which will provide a good guide as to how this method works.

James Balfour Paul wrote an introduction to Margaret Stuart's *Scottish family history*, published in 1930, in which he describes various approaches to writing a family history. The anecdotal method is usually quite easy to read, being chatty and amusing. It does not normally include many references to sources of information and does not quote from these sources to any great extent. The historical method attempts to place the family in its historical context, looking at how historical events affected the family and, perhaps, what impact the family made on history. The most comprehensive approach he calls the scientific method in which all the available facts are recorded, full references to sources are provided and sources are quoted at length, possibly in a second volume containing only extracts from source materials.

You will have to make your own decision about which approach or combination of approaches you wish to take, but we would certainly hope that you would include an element of the historical method in whatever you decide upon. No family exists in a vacuum, and knowledge of the community and environment in which it lived is vitally important in reaching a proper understanding of its history. By placing the family in historical context, you can pick out features which your family had in common with its surrounding community and also those features which were different. This type of approach may also help your family history appeal to local historians and others who may then be able to draw on your work to assist them with their own endeavours on a larger scale. Whatever methods you employ to write up your family history, there are a number of important points to be considered.

• You may need to decide whether to impose *censorship* on the material to be included in your history. Perhaps this will depend on who is likely to be reading the end product, but it could be that certain stories or facts gathered in the course of your researches would cause offence, so it is something worth thinking about.

• It is helpful to have clear in your mind a *procedure* for describing the history of the various branches of your family, since without a clear structure, the history could become very confusing to everyone but yourself. The best plan is to begin with the earliest known ancestor, giving his story, including information about his wife or wives and children as they appear in the course of his life. After giving his date of death, repeat the names of his wife and children and also give brief details about any of them who will not be described more fully later. For those to be mentioned again, it is useful to quote after their names the pages referring to them. In most cases it is probably best to complete one line of descent down to the most recent family members as one chapter and then consider other branches in later sections of the history.

• There are a number of features which you can use to improve the clarity of your account while adding to its interest. Most important here are *family tree charts*. For a large and complicated family history you might need a main chart supplemented by others for each branch of the family. Only very brief details will be required on the charts since the individuals will be fully described in the text, but you may want to indicate the page numbers of the individuals' entries against their names on the chart.

• An *index and table of contents* are also very worthwhile if the finished work is of reasonable length. Be careful to make it very clear in the index which particular person is being referred to, since so often there will be several family members with the same name. You could use dates, places of residence and occupations to distinguish between them.

• References to your sources of information should be included to either a lesser or greater extent depending on your viewpoint. To avoid interrupting the flow of your narrative, use numbers in the text, with the corresponding notes appearing at the foot of the page or at the end of either the chapter or the whole work.

• Illustrations will obviously increase the interest of your work and so, if possible, you should include pictures of members of the family, of places where they lived, were educated and worked, churches where they were baptised and married, tombstones, medals and perhaps even coats of arms.

• Although your researches will have gathered plenty of information about the members of your family, for the purposes of a family history, particularly one using the 'historical method', you will need to build up some background information on the national and local history of the time. This should include not only events but also the social and economic conditions that would affect your family. You could use a chronology such as Steinberg's *Historical tables* to identify events of national importance. Otherwise, consult national and local histories, social and economic histories and, where appropriate, histories of occupations and institutions with which family members were associated, such as churches, schools and universities. The best place to seek advice on what sources are available is the local history or local studies section of the libary for the area you are interested in. Particularly important sources for local history are the three series of Statistical Accounts of Scotland, with a section devoted to each parish in Scotland. The '*Old*' *Statistical Account*, published 1791–1799 and the *New Statistical Account* of 1845, have entries written by the parish ministers and vary greatly in length, depending on the interests of each minister. The *Third Statistical Account*, 1951–1992, was written by a variety of contributors regarded as being knowledgeable about specific areas, but is probably, at present, of less value to family historians than the two earlier 'accounts'. The relevant sections should certainly be regarded as 'essential reading' for anyone writing a family history. It is worthwhile putting some effort into this background research and it should help you to produce a much better end product. This will allow you to produce a real history of your family in historical context as opposed to a mere chronicle of family events.

### Other formats

Since today it is easy to make use of various media, you might want to try your hand at using audio cassette recordings, tape/slide presentations or video recordings to give your family history an added dimension. Perhaps you have already used audio cassettes to record relatives' reminiscences, and some local libraries keep collections of oral history recorded in this format. Extracts could be used to make up a cassette to accompany the text of your history; the audio equivalent of a second volume containing extracts from sources, as mentioned earlier.

Tape/slide presentations and video recordings could be used as an additional feature of a family history or, with a lot of planning, the whole work might be produced in one of these formats. Obviously there is scope here ranging from a fairly basic presentation to a very ambitious production depending on your talents in this field. You may well not feel the need or inclination to venture into any media other than the written word, but we mention these as possibilities which not long ago would have been impracticable.

CHAPTER 8

# *Widening the Net*

## Introduction

Although it is always preferable, and more exciting, to carry out your family history research on site and under your own control, very often this is just not practicable. Amongst other things this chapter aims to show you how you can still carry out research even though you cannot make direct contact with the primary sources of the information.

There are a number of ways in which you can tap into sources of information, either by access to libraries, by means of correspondence with others with similar interests, by membership of appropriate family history societies, or (a recent development) by accessing, through a computer, appropriate information on the Internet.

## Genealogical directories

There are a few publications of this type, such as the annually published *International Genealogical Directory*.

Amongst other items, these usually contain a listing of each subscriber's interests, and a directory of the subscribers' addresses. Naturally, the larger international directories are potentially of greater value, as the scope of coverage increases the likelihood that there will be someone else interested in the same surname in the same geographical area as yourself. It is usually possible to write to the person listed, enclosing some information from your own research, and requesting some information from your correspondent's research in return.

By this means, one of the authors made contact with his mother's Hulson family members, of whom no living relatives were known prior to that contact made through the genealogical directory. Furthermore, a family history was traced back to the early part of the eighteenth century. Prior to that lucky contact by means of a genealogical directory, the only information that the author knew was his grandfather's name and the date of his death within about five years.

Of course, this is largely a matter of good fortune. Nevertheless, developing an interesting family history is dependent upon the fortuitous tracing of links. It just goes to show that every feasible and legitimate way of finding contacts should be pursued by the ambitious family history hunter!

### Magazines or journals for family historians

Such publications include *Family History* (published by the Institute of Heraldic & Genealogical Studies), *Family Tree magazine* and *Computers in Genealogy*.

These magazines and journals will contain articles of topical interest to the budding genealogist, and usually provide guidance on a variety of aspects of, or approaches to, tracing your family tree. In addition, there could be sections devoted to advertising personal interests, and the sharing of information with others seeking similar information. Frequently adverts are placed in such magazines by those willing (for a variable, but usually reasonable, fee) to undertake some research in particular areas of the country – this may be of value to you if, for any reason, you are unable to travel to the area in person.

## Family history societies

There is a considerable, and growing, number of societies throughout the UK. These societies are set up with the purpose of promoting family history research, most commonly in a specific geographical area. Meetings are usually held on a regular basis, with guest speakers, and most societies will publish their own newsletter. In most cases, the society will co-ordinate some projects, such as the transcription of monumental inscriptions in its own area, together with other specific projects from time to time.

There is a national overseeing body, the Federation of Family History Societies, which is in Birmingham. This society produces a series of very useful booklets on various aspects of family history.

It is worth joining your local society in order to meet others who share your hobby. In addition, it can be very worthwhile to join the society related to the local area of your ancestors. Local Family History Societies have readier access to some items of particular local interest, and their members, with the benefit of local knowledge, can be very helpful to you in your research.

A relevant address list is provided in the appendices.

Very many Scots have ancestors from England or Ireland and so the following two sections may be of some help in highlighting some differences between the records of these countries and those of Scotland.

## English Records

The Civil Registers in England do begin earlier (1837),

but provide less information. For example, the marriage certificates give only the names of the fathers of the bride and groom and the death certificates do not give any parents names at all.

The procedure for searching the Civil Registers is also quite different. The indexes only are available at the Family Records Centre in London and if you find an entry which you are interested in, you must then apply for an official copy of the certificate. Searching in this way can take very much longer than a day's general search in New Register House, where you can verify entries as you go.

There is little to say about the Census records since these are virtually the same and are also kept in the Family Records Centre. As in Scotland, there is an index to the 1881 Census, which is available on microfiche.

The IGI is available on microfiche divided up by county and on CD-ROM for the U.K. as a whole.

When we come to the earlier records, we see a contrast between the centralisation of many of the Scottish sources in New Register House and the Scottish Record Office and the decentralisation in England and Wales, with much being kept in the local archives or record offices. In particular, the Parish Registers are held in the local offices. Many more of these have earlier starting dates than in Scotland, with 1538 or 1558 being fairly common.

Other major sources are Wills and Administrations, Marriage Licences and land records.

Wills and Administrations (granted for those not leaving a Will) from 1858 with indexes available in Somerset House are stored centrally in London. Before 1858 they may be found in several locations. For more information on how to locate these you could consult *Wills and their whereabouts* by A.J. Camp. The Prerogative Court of Canterbury Wills are now kept at the Family Records Centre, London.

Marriage Licences : In Scotland, marriages were authorised by the proclamation of banns, but in England there was the alternative of having a marriage licence granted. These are found mainly in local archives or record offices and some have been published. Often they give the occupation of the groom and name the place or places where the marriage might take place. In a situation where one or both of the couple were under age, the consent of the parents would be required and so in most cases the father's name would be given.

Land records : These are nothing like as complete as in Scotland. The main sources are the Manorial Court Rolls which have survived for some areas, but are haphazard compared to the Sasines.

## Irish Records

To begin with, the bad news. Unfortunately many Irish records were lost in 1922 when the Four Courts in Dublin were destroyed. Amongst these were almost all Irish wills and about 1,000 Protestant church registers of baptisms, marriages and burials. Now let's look at what does survive.

Civil Registration began in 1864, giving the same information as English Civil Registration but Protestant marriages had been registered from 1845. All these records are in the General Register Office of Ireland in Dublin, except for the Civil Registers covering Northern Ireland from 1922, which are in the General Register Office (Northern Ireland) in Belfast.

Census records: unlike the rest of the British Isles, the Census records for 1901 and 1911 are open to the public and fairly complete, but before this, little exists. Lists of what there is appear in *Handbook on Irish genealogy* edited by D.F. Begley (1984).

All Census records are held in the National Archives in Dublin.

Church registers: the coverage of Church registers is not good, with only a few Roman Catholic registers from before 1820. There are microfilm copies of these in the National Library of Ireland, Dublin. For the Church of Ireland, the Irish branch of the Anglican Church, about 600 registers have survived and are held by the local churches, or in the National Archives, Dublin. It is advisable to check with the Church of Ireland in Dublin for further details. Many of the Presbyterian Church records are held by either the local churches or the Presbyterian Historical Society in Belfast.

Wills: although very many of these were destroyed, the situation is not quite as bad as it might seem at first. There is an index published in 1897 entitled Index to the Prerogative Wills of Ireland, 1536–1810 by Vicars and also the Betham extracts of wills – extracts of genealogical information from almost all wills proved in the Prerogative Court of Armagh, 1536–1800. These are mainly confined to wills of those with property in more than one diocese. There are copies of these extracts in the National Archives, Dublin and the Genealogical Office, also in Dublin. Various other abstracts and lists of wills which existed are also available, including some of diocesan wills. From 1858 onwards there are indexes of Wills and Administrations in the National Archives in Dublin, giving the date of death of the individual along with the names and addresses of the executors. Finally, copies and extracts of many Ulster wills are preserved in the Public Record Office of Northern Ireland.

Marriage licences: the Prerogative Marriage Licences for 1630–1858 and the Ossory Consistory Licences, 1734–1808 are kept in the Genealogical Office, in Dublin. Indexes for about a dozen dioceses, covering the period up to 1857 are available in the National Archives in Dublin while some have been printed up to 1800.

Register of Deeds: this is held in the Registry of Deeds, Dublin and includes records of the transfer of land since 1708 rather similar to the Sasines. It is indexed by names (grantors only) and places. The Register also includes other transactions which involved land, such as marriage settlements, mortgages, etc.

Monumental inscriptions: as in Scotland, many inscriptions have been recorded and published and can prove a useful source.

## Emigration and Immigration

Although there has been both emigration from and immigration into Scotland on a fairly large scale, there are very few records of this movement of population. There are ship passenger lists, but these only commence in 1890 and are in the Public Record Office in London. If your interest lies in emigrants before this date, as is more than likely, there are several published lists covering emigrants to Canada and the United States, which have been compiled from various sources and are listed in the Further reading and sources list. Having checked these, your next course of action would be to consult the immigration records of the country of destination.

During the first half of the nineteenth century in particular there was a considerable influx of Irish people into Scotland, with the main destinations being Glasgow, Edinburgh and Dundee. It can be very difficult to trace the place of origin of these immigrants since the Census records only record the birthplace as Ireland. The most useful source is the Poor Relief Applications which record the birthplaces of many Irish in Scotland, and this gives an added value to the Database in the Glasgow City Archives since Glasgow had the largest concentration of Irish in Scotland.

## Clans

One of the main traditions associated with Scotland is that of the clans. These were communities who owed allegiance to a chief, and many of the members claimed descent from a common ancestor although some associated themselves with a particular clan to receive its protection. They did not all necessarily share the same surname. Geographically the clans are mainly identified with the Highlands and Borders of Scotland, but many of their present-day attributes are accretions of the nineteenth and twentieth centuries.

As far as the family historian is concerned, the tradition of the clans probably has little significance beyond the fact that it has encouraged the production of clan histories. These will usually give plenty of information about the chief and his family but probably not a great deal about the ordinary clansmen. You may find them useful in providing some background information about the social, economic and political situation affecting the clan and the locality in which it was based. There are also many clan Societies and Associations which may help you contact others with similar genealogical interests to your own.

## The Internet and family history

This is a very new and rapidly developing source of information for the family historian. At the time of writing the information is in a state of constant change. Some of the information is quite volatile – it may appear one week and disappear the next, only to reappear in another form the following week. Some information may disappear entirely, whilst other new and more valuable resources will replace it.

This latest facility which the use of computers offers to

the family historian, provides the ability to communicate with others and access information by means of the Internet. Details of how to link up to the Internet are not the province of this book – there are many sources of information on the technical details – from commercial adverts to computer magazine articles and textbooks.

## E-mail

The use of e-mail can allow you to communicate quite simply with individuals, or a group of people, interested in family history. It is also possible to link up with newsgroups by means of the e-mail system. One of the most commonly known ones is a mailing list for United Kingdom and Ireland Genealogy – known as GENBRIT.

A sample of the kind of information which appears is as follows:

Date: Fri, 7 Feb 1997 02:22:10 -0500
Reply-To: UK and Ireland Genealogy Discussion List <GENUKI-L@MAIL.EWORLD.COM> Sender: UK and Ireland Genealogy Discussion List <GENUKI-L@MAIL.EWORLD.COM> From: Automatic digest processor <LISTSERV@MAIL.EWORLD.COM> Subject: GENUKI-L Digest – 6 Feb 1997 to 7 Feb 1997 – Special issue To: Recipients of GENUKI-L digests <GENUKI-L@MAIL.EWORLD.COM>

There are 46 messages totalling 1011 lines in this issue.

Topics in this special issue:
1. would like to hear from Carlins who have traced their family to Ireland
2. HARLAND, Phila., PA, 1780
3. RMS ORFORD (2)
4. Gibson Guide (was: Re: Poor Rolls 1700's, 1800's)
5. RODDA – CROWAN, CON
6. TRAVIS
7. Pallot's Marriage Index
8. PHELPS;Hardwicke,Gls;1800–1850

9. PHELPS; Llanvihangel Ystern Llewern, Monm; 1830–1844
10. ?Scottish Naming Patterns (2)
11. RICE in Dublin today
12. Postal code for Greystones, Co. Wicklow, Ireland
13. 19C fares UK to      Australia
14. AKIN/EAKIN; NIR/SCT
15. How would I obtain information on my ancestor's company in London?
16. Scotland: Free Church vs. Established?
17. Sullivan IRE>MA>PA
18. Decipher Co Down Place Name? (2)
19. Packet Ship Halifax
20. Search for Scotish relative
21. Snail mail correspondence
22. HELP NEEDED WITH DURHAM RESEARCH
23. YELLOOO
24. Cost of BDM
25. Stoke Newington-streets
26. Surname Love
27. A Watch from Queen Victoria
28. Stratford – which one????
29. BUCKS – which society do I join?
30. Timothy Connor (or O'Connor)
31. PARTINGTON, Ralph
32. phone fee for Internet use
33. Davis from Wales to New York
34. Help with Scottish geography lesson. 35. LENMAR & Rachel Florence      KINDON
36. POYTHRESS Joshua, London, ENG; b.1588 37. www.netwales.co.uk
38. Any records of Jersey CHI school teachers c1850? 39. Derivation of the      Name "Sybella"
40. BANKS of Lymington, HAMPSHIRE
41. M.SEALE OF GALWAY
42. MOJE
43. Maps-Ireland

---

There are also lists for interest in particular surnames. One of the best known is the American-based ROOTS surnames list. A sample of the kind of information which appears is as follows:

New entries are marked by a +, modified entries by a *, and expiring entries by an x. Clicking on the highlighted code words will give the name and address of the researcher who submitted the surname. (If no names are listed below this line, then none were found.)

```
Ramsay   1716   1892 SCT>PA>MD,USA gryphon
Ramsay   1720   1740 Leuchars,FIF,SCT lesleyr
Ramsay   1790   1850 SCT maryr
Ramsay   1790   1874 ANS,SCT>Dornoch,SUT,SCT jk
Ramsay   1798   1850 AugustaCo,VA,USA reese
Ramsay   1799   1946 PER,SCT>FIF,SCT>PER,SCT lynne
Ramsay   1820   now SCT>ZAF dramsay
Ramsay   1834   1885 PollamoreNear, CAV,IRL>NewYork,
                 NY,USA drm
Ramsay   1835   1898 Dornoch,SUT,SCT>AUS>
                 Otago,NZL jk
Ramsay   1840   1926 MLN,SCT johnb
Ramsay   1840   1981 SCT>CA>PierceCo,WA,USA traff
Ramsay   1846   1920 RenfrewCo,ON,CAN mklathem
Ramsay   1914   1980 Nanaimo,BC,CAN>CA>WA,
                 USA mecum
Ramsay   1700s  —— Nunlands,/Foulden,BEW,SCT
                 bbowyer
Ramsay   c1720  1747 DUR,ENG bpears
Ramsay   c1760  1996 DUR,ENG>IL>IA,USA lyles
Ramsay   c1770  now
Campbelltown,Kintyre,ARL,SCT>PE,
                 CAN milligf
Ramsay – see Ramsey (aet)
Ramsay – see Ramsey (yarb)
```

------------------------------------------------------------

Surname (required)
Location (optional, enter province, state or country abbreviation)

------------------------------------------------------------

There is a table of abbreviations. Or you can return to the main RSL page or to the RootsWeb home page.
------------------------------------------------------------©

Mount Pinos Webspinners — 02 February 1997
Webspinner@rootsweb.com

*The World Wide Web*

The World Wide Web provides you with a way to look at pages of information on the computer screen, placed there by many different people and organisations from all over the world. Again, the technicalities of using 'the Web' are not the province of this book. However, a large and ever-increasing set of sources of information are accessible on the WWW, which could be of interest to the family historian.

Some kinds of information 'published' on the Web include guides, hints on genealogy and information on sources (including types of information and the dates covered). Also available by this means are addresses of archives, record offices and family history societies. A new area of growth is the provision of searchable on-line databases, and individuals have also published their own information on their 'home pages'.

If there is something of particular interest to you, it is possible to search for it on the WWW. There are particularly powerful 'Search Engines' available – such as Magellan, Excite, Yahoo and AltaVista which will make the search relatively straightforward. Once you have found a 'site' of recurrent interest it is possible to keep an electronic 'bookmark', to save the bother of carrying out another search.

*Searchable on-line databases*

The increasing availability of these databases on the Internet will enable the family historian to carry out some research directly through the Internet. Although, at the time of writing, there is very little available which covers Scottish material, this will probably change in the near future.

One source already on-line which you might find useful is the National Register of Archives (NRA) database.

Although the NRA is based in London, it receives reports from the National Register of Archives (Scotland), and so some Scottish material is included, although less detail is provided than in the full surveys of the NRA (Scotland). As described in Chapter 6, these list original sources held outwith the Scottish Record Office. By using this on-line database, you may quickly be able to track down an elusive source and then contact the NRA(S) for further details of where the records are kept.

As mentioned earlier, the Scottish Record Office is developing a 'Gifts & Deposits Textbase' and a National Register of Archives (Scotland) Textbase. These databases, along with others currently being created for internal use in the SRO, may eventually be available on the Internet, although nothing is definite at this stage.

In the very near future, New Register House will make the indexes of births, marriages and deaths from 1855 to 1897, the index of the 1891 Census and the indexes to the baptisms and marriages in the 'Old' Parish Registers, available on the Internet, with appropriate charges. There are longer term plans to include the index of the 1881 Census.

There follows a list of some possible sources of genealogical information on the World Wide Web (WWW):

## Some Sources of Family History on the Internet

### Scotland
Angus Archives.
> http://www.angus.gov.uk/history/history.htm

Ayrshire Archives.
> http://www.south-ayrshire.gov.uk/Archives/
> Default.htm

Dundee City Archives and Record Centre.
> http://www.taynet.co.uk/users/scotgensoc/

The Gathering of the Clans.
  http://www.tartans.com/

Glasgow City Archives.
  http://users.colloquium.co.uk/~glw_archives/
  src001.htm

Glasgow University Archives and Business Records Centre.
  http://www.arts.gla.ac.uk/Archives/arcbrc.htm
  Details of holdings of University Archives,Greater
  Glasgow Health Board Archive, Business Records
  Centre and Scottish Brewing Archive.
Scottish Genealogy Society.
  http://www.taynet.co.uk/users/scotgensoc/


## Ireland

IRLGEN : Genealogical guide to Ireland.
  http://www.bess.tcd.ie/roots/prototyp/
  genweb2.htm
  Details of sources for Irish genealogy, based on :
  Tracing your Irish ancestors / John Grenham. Gill and
  Macmillan, 1992.

The National Archives of Ireland. (Dublin)
  http://www.kst.dit.ie/nat-arch/genealogy.html
  Information on Irish family history and genealogy.
  Includes Transportation Records for 1788–1868,
  to Australia.
  S

North of Ireland Family History Society.
  http://www.os.qub.ac.uk/nifhs/
  Includes 1851 Census fragments for Co Antrim
  S

PRO of Northern Ireland.
  http://proni.nics.gov.uk/index.htm
  General information and fairly full details of holdings..

## United Kingdom and Ireland
GENUKI home page.
  http://midas.ac.uk/genuki/
  General information on sources, addresses of record
  offices, etc. for genealogy in the United Kingdom and
  Ireland.

Public Record Office.
  http://www.open.gov.uk/pro/prohome.htm
  Fairly general information on the holdings of the PRO.
  An E-mail service exists.
Ron Taylor's UK Census finding aids and indexes.
  http://rontay.digiweb.com/
  Includes some small searchable databases, still being
  developed.
  **S**

Royal Commission on Historical Manuscripts
  http://www.hmc.gov.uk/
  Includes the National Register of Archives. Can be
  accessed directly if there is a telnet program running
  underneath the Web browser. Otherwise type:-
  telnet public.hmc.gov.uk
  **S**

Sociey of Genealogists
  http://boulmer.ncl.ac.uk/genuki/SoG/index.html

UK Archival Repositories on the Internet.
  http://www.liv.ac.uk/~spw1/uksites.htm
  Very useful listing of record offices, universities, etc. in
  the United Kingdom.

## International

Acadian Genealogy Homepage.
   http://www.acadian.org/
   French-Canadian genealogy.
   Over 1,000 genealogy related sites, including links to
   many personal homepages and other genealogy pages.

Cyndi's list of genealogy sites on the Internet.
   http://www.oz.net/~cyndihow/sites.htm
   A comprehensive listing of worldwide sites.

Everton's genealogical helper.
   http://www.everton.com/
   Based in U.S.A. Lists various databases to which you
   can subscribe, e.g. Family file, Pedigree file, Social
   Security Death Index (over 60 million names), 1851
   U.K. Census sample (500,000 entries), U.K. Marriage
   Witness List.
   **S** Also other links.

Online Genealogical Database Index
   http://www.gentree.com
   Based in the U.S.A. Claims to have links to all known
   genealogical  databases searchable through the WWW.
   These are mainly databases of particular families rather
   than of original sources and tend to be named after
   their author, which may not be a good indicator of the
   data they include.

RAND Genealogy Club.
   http://www.rand.org/personal/Genea/
   Based in the U.S.A. There are links to telephone
   directories and interesting databases on Royal families
   and medieval genealogy.

   **S** = searchable databases of primary sources.

# Forms for recording Information

The forms may be
photocopied for your own use.

# Family Questionnaire Form (page 1)

**Your Name:** _____ **Husband / Wife (& maiden name)** _____

(Please give full names & previous surname/s where appropriate)

Date & Place of Birth / Baptism _____

Date & Place of Marriage _____

Date & Place of Death / Burial _____

Occupation _____

**Your Children**

Date & Place of Birth / Baptism   1 _____ 2 _____ 3 _____

Date & Place of Marriage _____

Name of Husband / Wife _____

Date & Place of Death / Burial _____

Occupation _____

Their Children   1 _____ 2 _____ 3 _____

**Your Father** _____ **Your Mother (& maiden name)** _____

Name _____

Date & Place of Birth / Baptism _____

Date & Place of Marriage _____

Date & Place of Death / Burial _____

Occupation _____

108

# Family Questionnaire Form (page 2)

## Your FATHER's Father          His Wife (& maiden name)

Name _____          _____

Date & Place of Birth / Baptism _____          _____

Date & Place of Marriage _____

Date & Place of Death / Burial _____          _____

Occupation _____          _____

## Your MOTHER's Father          His Wife (& maiden name)

Name _____          _____

Date & Place of Birth / Baptism _____          _____

Date & Place of Marriage _____

Date & Place of Death / Burial _____          _____

Occupation _____          _____

**Your current address:** _____
_____
_____

**& telephone number:**

109

# Family Questionnaire Form (page 3)

## Other Family Members

*Do you know any other information about other relatives, such as uncles, aunts, great-uncles, great-aunts, cousins, etc....?*

1. Full name
   Details _____ Relationship _____

2. Full name _____ Relationship _____
   Details

3. Full name _____ Relationship _____
   Details

# Family Questionnaire Form

## Family Traditions

*Are there any family traditions / stories which you can recall?*

_____
_____
_____
_____
_____
_____
_____
_____
_____
_____
_____
_____
_____

*Do you know of the existence of a Family Bible?  Does it have family details?  Where is it?*

_____
_____
_____
_____

# Birth Certificate Details

First names:

Surname:

When:

Where:

Father's Name:

Father's Occupation:

Mother's Name:

Date of Marriage:
    (except 1856-61)
Informant:
    Qualification:
    Residence:

When registered:

Where registered:

Registrar:

---

First names:

Surname:

When:

Where:

Father's Name:

Father's Occupation:

Mother's Name:

Date of Marriage:
    (except 1856-61)
Informant:
    Qualification:
    Residence

When registered:

Where registered:

Registrar:

112

# Marriage Certificate Details

When, where and how           :

Name of 'GROOM               :
    Status                   :
    Occupation               :
    Age                      :
    Usual residence          :

Name of BRIDE                :
    Status                   :
    Occupation               :
    Age                      :
    Usual residence          :

Father of 'GROOM             :
    occupation               :
    Mother                   :

Father of BRIDE              :
    occupation               :
    Mother                   :

Minister / Registrar         :
    when & where             :

Witnesses                    :

---

When, where and how           :

Name of 'GROOM               :
    Status                   :
    Occupation               :
    Age                      :
    Usual residence          :

Name of BRIDE                :
    Status                   :
    Occupation               :
    Age                      :
    Usual residence          :

Father of 'GROOM             :
    occupation               :
    Mother                   :

Father of BRIDE              :
    occupation               :
    Mother                   :

Minister / Registrar         :
    when & where             :

Witnesses                    :

# Death Certificate Details

Name                        :
    occupation          :
    status              :
When                        :

Where                       :

Age:

Father's name               :
    occupation          :

Mother's name               :
    maiden name         :

Cause of death              :
    duration of disease :
    physician           :

Informant's name            :
    Qualification       :
    Residence           :

When registered             :
    Where               :
    Registrar           :

---

Name                        :
    occupation          :
    status              :
When                        :

Where                       :

Age:

Father's name               :
    occupation          :

Mother's name               :
    maiden name         :

Cause of death              :
    duration of disease :
    physician           :

Informant's name            :
    Qualification       :
    Residence           :

When registered             :
    Where               :
    Registrar           :

114

# Census Details Form

| Address | Name | Rein | M or S | Age | Occupation | Where Born |
|---------|------|------|--------|-----|------------|------------|
|         |      |      |        |     |            |            |
|         |      |      |        |     |            |            |
|         |      |      |        |     |            |            |
|         |      |      |        |     |            |            |
|         |      |      |        |     |            |            |
|         |      |      |        |     |            |            |
|         |      |      |        |     |            |            |
|         |      |      |        |     |            |            |
|         |      |      |        |     |            |            |
|         |      |      |        |     |            |            |
|         |      |      |        |     |            |            |
|         |      |      |        |     |            |            |
|         |      |      |        |     |            |            |
|         |      |      |        |     |            |            |
|         |      |      |        |     |            |            |
|         |      |      |        |     |            |            |
|         |      |      |        |     |            |            |
|         |      |      |        |     |            |            |
|         |      |      |        |     |            |            |
|         |      |      |        |     |            |            |

# IGI Index Details Form

| Person 1 | Person 2 | Person 3 | Sex | Type | Date | Parish |
|----------|----------|----------|-----|------|------|--------|
|          |          |          |     |      |      |        |
|          |          |          |     |      |      |        |
|          |          |          |     |      |      |        |
|          |          |          |     |      |      |        |
|          |          |          |     |      |      |        |
|          |          |          |     |      |      |        |
|          |          |          |     |      |      |        |
|          |          |          |     |      |      |        |
|          |          |          |     |      |      |        |
|          |          |          |     |      |      |        |
|          |          |          |     |      |      |        |
|          |          |          |     |      |      |        |
|          |          |          |     |      |      |        |
|          |          |          |     |      |      |        |
|          |          |          |     |      |      |        |
|          |          |          |     |      |      |        |
|          |          |          |     |      |      |        |
|          |          |          |     |      |      |        |
|          |          |          |     |      |      |        |
|          |          |          |     |      |      |        |
|          |          |          |     |      |      |        |
|          |          |          |     |      |      |        |
|          |          |          |     |      |      |        |

# APPENDIX B:

## *Useful Addresses*

## National records

Court of the Lord Lyon,
HM New Register House,
Edinburgh. EH1 3YT
Tel. 0131- 556 7255

General Register Office
(Scotland),
New Register House,
Edinburgh. EH1 3YT
Tel. 0131-334  0380

National Library of
Scotland,
George IV Bridge,
Edinburgh. EH1 1EW
Tel. 0131- 226 4531
    0131- 459 4531

National Register of
Archives (Scotland),
HM General Register
House,
Edinburgh. EH1 3YY
Tel. 0131- 535 1403

Registers of Scotland,
Cowglen Office,
National Savings Bank
Building,
Boydstone Road,
Glasgow. G53 6RS
Tel. 0141-306 4400

Registrar of Births, Deaths
& Marriages,
Commercial Street,
Dundee
DD1 2AF
Tel. 01382 - 435222

Registrar of Births, Deaths
& Marriages,
22 Park Circus,
Glasgow.
Tel. 0141-287  8350

Scottish Jewish Archives
Centre,
Garnethill Synagogue,
125–127 Hill Street,
Glasgow. G3
Tel. 0141- 332 4911

Scottish Record Office,
HM General Register
House,
Edinburgh. EH1 3YY
Tel. 0131-535 1314

West Register House,
Charlotte Square,
Edinburgh. EH2 4DP

William Coull Anderson
Library of Genealogy,
Dewar House,
Hill Terrace,
Arbroath. DD11 1AJ
Tel. 01241- 872248

## Mormon Church
(Church of Jesus Christ of
Latter-Day Saints) Family
History Libraries

*Aberdeen*
LDS Chapel,
North Anderson Drive,
Aberdeen.
Tel. 01224- 692206

*Dumfries*
LDS Chapel,
Albanybank, Dumfries.
Tel. 01387- 54865

*Dundee*
LDS Chapel,
Bingham Terrace,
Dundee.
Tel. 01382- 451247

*Edinburgh*
LDS Chapel,
30A Colinton Road,
Edinburgh.
Tel. 0131- 337 3049

*Glasgow*
LDS Chapel,
Julian Avenue,
Glasgow.
Tel. 0141- 357 1024
     0141- 945 1902

*Inverness*
LDS Chapel,
13 Ness Walk,
Inverness.
Tel. 01463- 231220

*Irvine*
LDS Chapel,
Banks Street,
Irvine, Ayrshire.
Tel. 01294- 273046

*Johnstone*
LDS Chapel,
Campbell Street,
Johnstone,
Renfrew.
Tel. 01505- 320886

*Kilmarnock*
LDS Chapel,
Whatriggs Road,
Kilmarnock, Ayrshire.
Tel. 01563- 28009

*Kirkcaldy*
LDS Chapel,
Winifred Crescent,
Forth Park, Kirkcaldy,
Fife.
Tel. 01592- 640041

## Local collections

*Aberdeen City Council*
Aberdeen City Archives
Branch,
Old Aberdeen House,
Dunbar Street,
Aberdeen. AB2 1UE
Tel. 01224-481775

The Charter Room
The Town House
Aberdeen AB10 1AQ
Tel. 01224-522513

*Angus Council*
Angus Archives,
Montrose Library,
214 High Street,
Montrose. DD10 8HE
Tel. 01674- 671415

*Argyll and Bute Council*
Argyll and Bute Council,
Manse Brae,
Lochgilphead. PA31 8QU
Tel. 01546-604120

*Ayrshire Council*
Ayrshire Archives,
County Buildings,
Wellington Square,
Ayr. KA7 1DR
Tel. 01292- 612138

*Borders Council*
Scottish Borders Archive
and Local History Centre,
St. Mary's Mill,
Selkirk. TD7 5EW
Tel. 01750- 20842

*Dumfries & Galloway Council*
Dumfries Archive Centre,
33 Burns Street,
Dumfries. DG1 2PS
Tel. 01387-269254

*Dundee City Council*
Dundee City Archive and
Record Centre, Support
Centre, 21 City Square,
Dundee. DD1 3BY
Tel. 01382- 434494

Search Room,
1 Shore Terrace, Dundee
Tel. 01382- 434494

*Edinburgh City Council*
City of Edinburgh Council
Archives, City Chambers,
High Street,
Edinburgh. EH1 1YJ
Tel. 0131-529 4616

Edinburgh Room,
Edinburgh City Libraries,

Central Library,
George IV Bridge,
Edinburgh. EH1 1EG
Tel. 0131- 225 5584

*Falkirk Council*
Falkirk Archives,
Callendar House Museum
and History Research Centre,
Falkirk FK1 1YR
Tel. 01324- 503770

*Glasgow Archdiocese*
*(Roman Catholic)*
The Archivist,
Archdiocese of Glasgow
Curial Offices,
196 Clyde Street,
Glasgow. G1 JY
Tel. 0141- 226 5898 extn.
154

*Glasgow City Council*
Glasgow City Archives,
Mitchell Library, North
Street, Glasgow. G3 7DN
Tel. 0141-287 2910

History and Glasgow Room,
Mitchell Library,
201 North Street,
Glasgow. G3 7DN
Tel. 0141-287 2937

*Highland Council*
Highland Council Archives,
Inverness Branch Library,
Farraline Park,
Inverness. IV1 1NH
Tel. 01463- 220330

North Highland Archives,
Carnegie Library,
Sinclair Terrace,
Wick. KW1 5AB
Tel. 01955- 606432

*Midlothian Council*
Midlothian Council Archives,
Library Headquarters,
2 Clerk Street,
Loanhead. EH20 9DR
Tel. 0131-440 2210

*Moray Council*
Moray Record Office,
Tolbooth, High Street,
Forres. IV36 0AB
Tel. 01309-673617

*North Lanarkshire Council*
North Lanarkshire Archives,
10 Kelvin Road,
Lenziemill,
Cumbernauld. G67 2BD
Tel. 01236- 737114

*Orkney Council*
Orkney Archives,
Orkney Library,
Laing Street,
Kirkwall. KW15 1NW
Tel. 01856- 873166

*Perth and Kinross Council*
Perth and Kinross Council
Archive,
A.K. Bell Library,
2–8 York Place,
Perth. PH2 8EP
Tel. 01738- 477022

*Shetland Council*
Shetland Archives,
44 King Harald Street,
Lerwick. ZE1 0EQ
Tel. 01595- 696247

*South Lanarkshire Council*
South Lanarkshire Archives,
Records Management Unit,
30 Hawbank Road,
College Milton,
East Kilbride
Tel. 01355- 239193

*Stirling Council*
Stirling Council Archives
Services,
Unit 6,
Burghmuir Industrial Estate,
Stirling. FK7 7PY
Tel. 01786-450745

*West Lothian Council*
West Lothian Council,
Archives & Records
Management Unit,
7 Rutherford Square,
Brucefield Industrial Estate,
Livingston. EH54 9BU
Tel. 01506- 460020

## Medical records

Dumfries and Galloway
Health Board Archives,
Crichton Royal Hospital,
Dumfries.
Tel. 01387- 255301

Greater Glasgow Health
Board Archive,
University of Glasgow,
Glasgow. G12 8QQ
Tel. 0141- 330 5516

Lothian Health Board,
Medical Archives Centre,
Edinburgh University
Library,
George Square,
Edinburgh. EH8 9LJ
Tel. 0131- 667 1011

Northern Health Services
Archives,
Aberdeen Royal Infirmary,
Woolmanhill,
Aberdeen. AB1 1LD
Tel. 01224- 663 456
       extn. 55562
       01224- 663 123

Royal College of Physicians
and Surgeons of Glasgow,
234-242 St. Vincent Street,
Glasgow. G2 5RJ
Tel. 0141- 221 6072

Royal College of Physicians
of Edinburgh,
9 Queen Street,
Edinburgh. EH2 1JQ
Tel. 0131- 225 7324

Royal College of Surgeons
of Edinburgh,
18 Nicolson Street,
Edinburgh. EH8 9DW
Tel. 0131- 556 6206

## Occupational records

Advocates' Library,
Parliament House,
Edinburgh. EH1 1RF
Tel. 0131- 226 5071

The Archivists,
Bank of Scotland,
Head Office,
The Mound,
Edinburgh. EH1 1YZ
Tel. 0131- 243 5467

The Archivist,
Royal Bank of Scotland,
42 St. Andrews Square,
Edinburgh. EH2 2AD
Tel. 0131- 556 7001

Signet Library,
Parliament Square,
Edinburgh. EH1 1RF
Tel. 0131- 225 4923

University of Glasgow
Archives,
Business Records Centre,
13 Thurso Street,
Glasgow. G11 6PE
Tel. 0141- 330 5516
       0141- 339 8855
       extn. 4543

# English records

Family Records Centre,
1 Myddelton Street,
London.
EC1R 1UW
Tel. 0181- 392 5300

Postal Application Section,
Office for National
Statistics,
Smedley Hydro,
Trafalgar Road,
Birkdale,
Southport,
Merseyside. PR8 2HH
Tel. 0151- 471 4800

Principal Registry (Family
Division),
Somerset House,
London. WC2R 1LP
Tel. 0171- 936 6000

Public Record Office,
Ruskin Avenue,
Kew, Richmond,
Surrey. TW9 4DU
Tel. 0181- 876 3444

# Irish records

### *Republic of Ireland*
Genealogical Office,
2 Kildare Street,
Dublin 2.
Tel. 6618811
(incorporating Office of the
Chief Herald and State
Heraldic Museum)

The General Register
Office,
Joyce House,
8–11 Lombard Street East,
Dublin 2.
Tel. 6711000

National Archives,
Bishop Street,
Dublin 8.
Tel. 4783711
(merger of the Public
Record Office and State
PaperOffice)

National Library,
Kildare Street,
Dublin 2.
Tel. 6618811

Registry of Deeds,
Henrietta Street,
Dublin 1.
Tel. 8732233

### *Northern Ireland*
General Register Office,
Oxford House,
49-55 Chichester Street,
Belfast. BT1 4HL
Tel. 01232- 235211

Presbyterian Historical
Society,
Room 218,
Church House,
Fisherwick Place,
Belfast. BT1 6DW
Tel. 01232- 323936

Public Record Office
(Northern Ireland),
66 Balmoral Avenue,
Belfast. BT9 6NY
Tel. 01232- 251318

## Societies and Associations

Aberdeen and North East
Scotland Family History
Society,
The Hon. Secretary,
The Family History Shop,
164 King Street,
Aberdeen. AB24 5BD
Tel. 01224- 646323

Anglo Scottish Family
History Society,
The Hon. Secretary,
c/o Manchester &
Lancashire Family History
Society,
Clayton House,
Manchester. M21 2AQ

Association of Scottish
Genealogists and Record
Agents (ASGRA),
The Hon. Secretary, James
A. Thomson,
84 Gilmore Place,
Edinburgh. EH3 9PF

Borders Family History
Society,
The Hon. Secretary,
15 Edinburgh Road,
Greenlaw,
Berwickshire. TD10 6XF

Catholic Family History
Society,
The Hon. Secretary,
2 Winscombe Crescent,
Ealing,
London. W5 1AZ

Central Scotland Family
History Society,
The Hon. Secretary,
29 Craiginnan Gardens,
Dollar,
Clackmannanshire.
FK14 7JA

Dumfries and Galloway
Family History Society,
Family History Centre,
9 Glasgow Street,
Dumfries. DG2 9AF

East Ayrshire Family
History Society,
c/o Dick Institute,
Elmbank Avenue,
Kilmarnock. KA1 3BU

Fife Family History Society,
The Hon. Secretary,
30 Duddingston Drive,
Kirkcaldy,
Fife. KY2 6JP

Glasgow and West of
Scotland Family History
Society,
The Hon. Secretary,
Unit 15,
32 Mansfield Street,
Glasgow. G11 5QP

Guild of One Name Studies,
The Hon. Secretary,
Box G, 14 Charterhouse
Buildings,
Goswell Road,
London. EC1M 7BA

Hamilton & District Family
History Society,
The Hon. Secretary,
83 Buchandykes Road,
Calderwood, East Kilbride,
Lanarkshire. G74 3BN

Highland Family History
Society,
The Hon. Secretary,
c/o Reference Room,
Public Library,
Farraline Park,
Inverness. IV1 1NH

Largs and North Ayrshire
Family History Society,
The Hon. Secretary,
13 Burnside Road, Largs,
Ayrshire. KA30 9BX

Midlothian Family History
Society,
Lasswade High School,
Eskdale Drive,
Bonnyrigg,
Midlothian. EH19 2LA

Scots Ancestry Research
Society,
29B Albany Street,
Edinburgh. EH1 3QN
Tel. 0131- 556 4220

Scottish Association of
Family History Societies,
Hon. Secretary, Alan J. L.
MacLeod,
51/3 Mortonhall Road,
Edinburgh. EH9 2HN

Scottish Genealogy Society,
Library & Family History
Centre, 15 Victoria Terrace,
Edinburgh. EH1 2JL
Tel. 0131- 220 3677

Shetland Family History
Society,
The Hon. Secretary,
12 Lovers Loan, Lerwick,
Shetland. ZE1 0ED

Society of Genealogists,
14 Charterhouse Buildings,
Goswell Road,
London. EC1M 7BA
Tel. 0171- 251 8799

Tay Valley Family History
Society,
The Hon. Secretary,
Family History Research
Centre, 179 Princes Street,
Dundee. DD4 6DQ
Tel. 01382- 461845

Troon and District Family
History Society,
The Hon. Secretary,
c/o M.E.R.C.,
Troon Public Library,
South Beach, Troon,
Ayrshire. KA10 6EF

# Further Reading and Sources

## General

**Burness, Lawrence R.** A Scottish genealogist's glossary. Aberdeen: Scottish Association of Family History Societies, 1991.

**Cairns-Smith-Barth, John Lawrence** Scottish family history: a research and source guide, volume 1: with particular emphasis on how to do your research from various sources available within Australia. Hampton, Vic.: Sue E. MacBeth Genealogical Books, 1986.

**Collins, Ewen K.** Beginner's guide to Scottish genealogy. Dundee: Tay Valley Family History Society, 1992.

**Colwell, Stella** The family history book: a guide to tracing your ancestors. Oxford: Phaidon, 1980.

**Communities** and families / edited by John Golby. Cambridge University Press in association with The Open University, 1994. (Studying family and community history: 19th and 20th centuries; volume 3)

**Cory, Kathleen B.** Tracing your Scottish ancestry. 2nd ed. Edinburgh: Polygon, 1996.

**Diack, H. Lesley** North east roots: a guide to sources. 3rd ed. Aberdeen: Aberdeen and N. E. Scotland Family History Society, 1996.

**FitzHugh, T. V. H.** The dictionary of genealogy. 3rd ed. London: A. & C. Black, 1991.

**From** family history to community history / edited by W. T. R. Pryce. Cambridge: Cambridge University Press in association with The Open University, 1994. (Studying family and community history: 19th and 20th centuries; volume 2)

**From** family tree to family history / edited by Ruth Finnegan and Michael Drake. Cambridge: Cambridge University Press in association with The Open University, 1994. (Studying family and community history: 19th and 20th centuries; volume 1)

**Hamilton-Edwards, Gerald** In search of ancestry. 4th ed. Sussex: Phillimore, 1983.

**Hamilton-Edwards, Gerald** In search of Scottish ancestry. 2nd rev. ed. Chichester: Phillimore, 1983.

**Hey, David** The Oxford companion to local and family history. Oxford: Oxford University Press, 1996.

**Hey, David** The Oxford dictionary of local and family history. Oxford: Oxford University Press, 1997.

**Hey, David.** The Oxford guide to family history. Oxford: Oxford University Press, 1993.

**James, Alwyn** Scottish roots: a step-by-step guide for ancestor hunters in Scotland and overseas. 2nd rev.ed. Edinburgh: Saltire Society, 1995.

**McLaughlin, Eve** No time for family history. 2nd ed. Birmingham: Federation of Family History Societies, 1992.

**Markwell, F. C. and Saul, P.** The family historian's 'enquire within.' 4th ed. Birmingham: Federation of Family History Societies, 1991.

**Miller, Susan** Strathclyde sources: a guide for family historians. 2nd ed. Glasgow: Glasgow & West of Scotland Family History Society, 1995.

**Moody, David** Scottish family history. London: Batsford, 1988.

**National** index of parish registers, vol.12: sources for Scottish genealogy and family history / edited by D. J. Steel. London: Phillimore, 1970.

**Perkins, J. P.** Current publications by member societies. 7th ed. Birmingham: Federation of Family History Societies, 1992.

**Practice** makes perfect: a workbook of genealogical exercises. Birmingham: Federation of Family History Societies, 1993.

**Sandison, Alexander** Tracing ancestors in Shetland. London: A. Sandison, 1985.

**Sinclair, Cecil** Tracing your Scottish ancestors: a guide to ancestry research in the Scottish Record Office. Edinburgh: HMSO, 1990.

**Sources** and methods for family and community historians: a handbook / edited by Michael Drake and Ruth Finnegan. Cambridge University Press in association with The Open

University, 1994. (Studying family and community history: 19th and 20th centuries; volume 4)

**Tay** Valley Family History Society source book. Dundee: Tay Valley Family History Society, 1988.

**Time,** family and community: perspectives on family and community history / edited by Michael Drake. Oxford: Blackwell in association with The Open University, 1994.

**Using** the past: audio-cassettes on sources and methods for family and community historians / edited by P. Braham. 6 audio-cassettes with notes. Milton Keynes: The Open University, 1993.

## Archives and record offices

**British** archives: a guide to archive resources in the United Kingdom / edited by J. Foster and J. Sheppard. London: HMSO, 1989.

**Cole, Jean and Church, Rosemary** In and around record repositories in Great Britain and Ireland. 3rd ed. Ramsey, Huntingdon: Family Tree Magazine, 1992.

**Cox, Jane M. and Padfield, Timothy R.** (revised Bevan and Duncan) Tracing your ancestors in the Public Record Office. 4th ed. London: HMSO, 1990.

**Gibson, Jeremy and Peskett, Pamela** Record offices: how to find them. 7th ed. Birmingham: Federation of Family History Societies, 1996.

**Guide** to the national archives of Scotland / Scottish Record Office. Edinburgh: The Stationery Office, 1996.

**Livingstone, M.** A guide to the public records of Scotland deposited in H. M. General Register House, Edinburgh. Edinburgh: H. M. General Register House, 1905.

**Record** repositories in Great Britain: a geographical directory / Royal Commission on Historical Manuscripts. 9th ed. London: HMSO, 1991.

**Sinclair, Cecil** Tracing your Scottish ancestors: a guide to ancestry research in the Scottish Record Office. Edinburgh: HMSO, 1990.

**Thomson, J. Maitland** The public records of Scotland. Glasgow: Maclehose, Jackson and co., 1922.

## Background information

**Mitchell, B. R.** British historical statistics. Cambridge: Cambridge University Press, 1988

**New** statistical account of Scotland. Edinburgh: W. Blackwood and Sons, 1845. 15 vols.

**Statistical** account of Scotland. Edinburgh: W. Creech, 1791–1799. 21 vols. (modern reprint available)

**Steinberg, S. H.** Historical tables, 58 BC–AD 1990. 12th ed. London: Macmillan, 1991.

**Third** statistical account of Scotland. [Various publishers], 1951–1992.

**Torrance, D. R.** Weights and measures for the Scottish family historian. Aberdeen: Scottish Association of Family History Societies, 1996.

## Bibliographies of Scotland

**Bibliography** of Scotland 1976– Edinburgh: National Library of Scotland, 1978–

**Bibliography** of Scotland on CD-ROM 1988– Edinburgh: National Library of Scotland, 1997– (This is also available, covering 1988 onwards, on the Internet via the National Library of Scotland homepage).

**Hancock, P. D.** A bibliography of works relating to Scotland 1916–1950. Edinburgh: Edinburgh University Press, 1959. 2 vols.

**Mitchell, Sir Arthur and Cash, C. G.** A contribution to the bibliography of Scottish topography. Edinburgh: Scottish History Society, 1917. 2 vols.

## Biographical dictionaries

**Anderson, William** The Scottish Nation. Edinburgh: A. Fullarton, 1875.

**Boase, Frederic** Modern English biography. Truro: Netherton and Worth, 1892–1921. 6 vols.

**British** biographical archive [on microfiche] London: K. G. Saur, 1984, 1991.

**Brown, James D. and Stratton, Stephen Samuel** British musical biography. Birmingham: Chadfield, 1897.

**Chambers, Robert** A biographical dictionary of eminent Scotsmen. London: Blackie, 1835 (and later editions).

**Chambers** Scottish biographical dictionary / editor: Rosemary Goring. London: Chambers, 1992.

**Dictionary** of business biography / edited by D. Jeremy and C. Shaw. London: Butterworth, 1984–1986. 5 vols. and supplement.

**Dictionary** of National Biography [Various publishers], 1885–

**Dictionary** of National Biography on CD-ROM. Oxford: Oxford University Press, 1995.

**Dictionary** of Scottish business biography, 1860–1960 / editors, Anthony Slaven, Sydney Checkland. Aberdeen: Aberdeen University Press, 1986, 1990. 2 vols.

**Eyre-Todd, George**
Who's who in Glasgow in 1909. Glasgow: Gowans & Gray, 1909.

**Saville, J. and Bellamy, J.** Dictionary of labour biography. London: Macmillan, 1992. 9 vols.

**Who** was who. London: A. & C. Black, 1897–. 9 vols. & index vol.

**Who's** who. London: A. & C. Black, 1849–

## Clans

**Adam, Frank** The clans, septs and regiments of the Scottish Highlands. 8th ed. revised by Sir T. Innes of Learney. Edinburgh and London: W. & A. K. Johnston & G. W. Bacon, 1970.

**Martine, R.** Scottish clan and family names: their arms, origins and tartans. Edinburgh: John Bartholomew, 1987.

## Computers

**Bayley, Nigel John** Computer aided genealogy: a guide to using computer software for family history. Farnborough, Hants.: S. & N. Publishing, 1995.

**Bradley, Alan** Family history on your P. C.: a book for beginners. Wilmslow, Cheshire: Sigma Press, 1996.

**Computers** in genealogy beginner's handbook / edited by N. C. Taylor. 2nd ed. London: Society of Genealogists, 1996.

**Drake, K.** Computer programs for the family historian on Amstrad PCW computers. Birmingham: Birmingham & Midland Society for Genealogy and Heraldry, 1996.

**Hawgood, David** Computers for family history. 5th rev. ed. London: D. Hawgood, 1994.

**Hawgood, David** GEDCOM data transfer: moving your family tree. London: Hawgood Computing Ltd., 1991.

**Hawgood, David** Genealogy computer packages. London: David Hawgood, 1993.

**Hawgood, David** Internet for genealogy. London: D. Hawgood, 1996.

**Hawgood, David** Introduction to using computers for genealogy. Birmingham: Federation of Family History Societies, 1994.

**Lawton, Guy** Spreadsheet family trees. London: D. Hawgood, 1994.

**Tippey, David** Genealogy on the Macintosh. London: David Hawgood, 1996.

## Current research

**International** genealogical directory Ferring, Sussex: Pinhorns, 1971-72–

**National** genealogical directory. Sussex: Michael J. Burchall and Judy Warren, 1979–

**Register** of one name studies. 11th ed. London: Guild of One-Name Studies, 1995.

## Education

**Craigie, James**
A bibliography of Scottish education before 1872 / James Craigie. London: University of London Press, 1970.

**Craigie, James**
A bibliography of Scottish education 1872–1972 / James Craigie. London: University of London Press, 1974.

**Jacobs, Phyllis M.** Registers of the universities, colleges and schools of Great Britain and Ireland. London: Athlone Press, 1964.

**Scottish** education bibliography 1970–1990 on CD-ROM / edited by Margaret Harrison. Glasgow: University of Strathclyde, Jordanhill Library, 1994.

*Aberdeen University*
**Fasti** academiae Mariscallanae Aberdonensis, 1593–1860 /

edited by Peter John Anderson and James Fowler Kellas Johnstone. Aberdeen: New Spalding Club, 1889–1898. 3 vols.

**Officers** and graduates of University and King's College, Aberdeen, 1495–1860 / edited by Peter John Anderson. Aberdeen: New Spalding Club, 1893.

**Roll** of alumni in Arts of the University and King's College of Aberdeen, 1596–1860 / edited by Peter John Anderson. Aberdeen: University of Aberdeen, 1900.

**Roll** of the graduates of the University of Aberdeen, 1860–1900 / [edited by] William Johnston. Aberdeen: University of Aberdeen, 1906.

**Roll** of the graduates of the University of Aberdeen 1901–1925; with supplement 1860–1900 / compiled by Theodore Watt. Aberdeen: Aberdeen University Press, 1935.

**Roll** of the graduates of the University of Aberdeen 1926–1955; with supplement 1860–1925 / compiled by John Mackintosh. Aberdeen: University of Aberdeen, 1960.

**Roll** of the graduates of the University of Aberdeen 1956–1970 with supplement 1860–1955 / [edited by] L. Donald and W. S. Maccdonald. Aberdeen: Aberdeen University Press, 1982.

### Glasgow University

The **matriculation** albums of the University of Glasgow from 1728 to 1858 / edited by W. Innes Addison. Glasgow: J. Maclehose and sons, 1913.

A **roll** of the graduates of the University of Glasgow from 1727 to 1897 / compiled by W. Innes Addison. Glasgow: J. Maclehose and sons, 1898.

### St. Andrews University

**Early** records of the University of St. Andrews: the graduate roll 1413–1579 and the matriculation roll 1473–1579 / edited by James Maitland Anderson. Edinburgh: Scottish History Society, 1926.

The **matriculation** roll of the University of St. Andrews, 1747–1897 / edited by James Maitland Anderson. Edinburgh: W. Blackwood and Sons, 1905.

## Emigration

**Dictionary** of Scottish emigrants into England and Wales. Manchester: Anglo-Scottish Family History Society, then Manchester & Lancashire Family History Society, 1984–1992. 5 vols.

**Dictionary** of Scottish emigrants to Canada before Confederation / edited by Donald Whyte. Toronto: Ontario Genealogical Society, 1986.

**Dictionary** of Scottish emigrants to the USA / edited by Donald Whyte. Baltimore: Magna Carta Books Co., 1972, 1986. 2 vols.

**Dictionary** of Scottish settlers in North America 1625–1825 / David Dobson. Baltimore: Genealogical Publishing Inc., 1985. 6 vols.

**Passenger** and immigration lists index: a guide to published arrival records of about 500,000 passengers in the United States and Canada / by P. William Filby and Mary K. Meyer. Detroit: Gale Research Co., 1981–1992.

## Heraldry

**Friar, Stephen** Heraldry for the local historian and genealogist. Gloucestershire: Alan Sutton, 1996.

**Innes of Learney, Sir Thomas** Scots heraldry. 2nd ed. Edinburgh: Oliver & Boyd, 1956.

**Paul, Sir James Balfour** An ordinary of arms contained in the Public Register of All Arms and Bearings (1672–1902), with Volume 2 (1903–1973) by David Reid of Robertland and Vivien Wilson. Edinburgh: Lyon Office, 1977.

**Swinnerton, Iain** Basic facts about heraldry for family historians. Birmingham: Federation of Family History Societies, 1995.

## Historical demography

**Glasgow**, volume II: 1830 to 1912 / edited by W. Hamish Fraser and Irene Maver. Manchester: Manchester University Press, 1996.

An **introduction** to English historical demography / edited by E. A. Wrigley. London: Weidenfeld & Nicolson, 1966.

**Macdonald, D, F**. Scotland's shifting population, 1770–1850. Glasgow: Jackson, Son and Co., 1937.

**Scottish** population history from the 17th century to the 1930s / edited by Michael Flinn. Cambridge: Cambridge University Press, 1977.

**Wrigley, E. A.** Identifying people in the past. London: Arnold, 1973.

## Indexes of family histories

**Barrow, Geoffrey B**. The genealogist's guide: an index to printed British pedigrees and family histories, 1950–1975. London: Research Publishing Co., 1977.

**Ferguson, Joan P. S.** Scottish family histories / compiled by Joan P. S. Ferguson. Edinburgh: National Library of Scotland, 1986.

**Grant, Francis J**. Index to genealogies, birthbriefs and funeral escutcheons recorded in the Lyon Office. Edinburgh: Scottish Record Society, 1908.

**Kaminkow, Marion J**. Genealogical manuscripts in British libraries: a descriptive guide. Baltimore: Magna Charta Book Co., 1967.

**Marshall, George W**. The genealogist's guide. (Reprinted from the last (4th ed.) of 1903) Baltimore: Genealogical Pub. Co., 1980.

**Stuart, Margaret** Scottish family history: a guide to works of reference on the history and genealogy of Scottish families. Edinburgh: Oliver and Boyd, 1930 (With an essay on how to write the history of a family, by Sir James Balfour Paul).

**Whitmore, J. B**. A genealogical guide: an index to British pedigrees in continuation of Marshall's Genealogist's guide, 1903. London: Walford Bros., 1953.

## Irish family history

**General** valuation of Ireland / Richard Griffith. Dublin: Her Majesty's Stationery Office, 1850–1861.

**Handbook** on Irish genealogy: how to trace your ancestors and relatives in Ireland / edited by Donal F. Begley. 6th ed. Dublin: Heraldic Artists, 1984.

**Index** to the Prerogative Wills of Ireland, 1536–1810 / edited by Sir Arthur Vicars. Dublin: E. Ponsonby, 1897.

**MacConghail, Máire and Gorry, Paul**. Tracing Irish ancestors. Glasgow: HarperCollins, 1997.

**Maxwell, Ian**; edited by Grace McGrath. Tracing your ancestors in Northern Ireland: a guide to ancestry research in the Public

Record Office of Northern Ireland. Edinburgh: The Stationery Office, 1997.

## Journals

**Computers** in genealogy [journal] London: Society of Genealogists, 1982–

**Family** history [journal] Canterbury: Institute of Heraldic and Genealogical Studies, 1962–

**Family** history news and digest [journal] Federation of Family History Societies, 1977–

**Family** tree magazine [journal] Huntingdon: Family Tree Magazine, 1984–

**Genealogical** periodical annual index. Bowie, Maryland: Heritage Books, 1962–

**Genealogists** magazine [journal] London: Society of Genealogists, 1925–

**Journal** of family history: studies in family, kinship and demography [journal] Greenwich, CT.: JAI Press Inc., 1976–

**Raymond, S. A.** British genealogical periodicals: a bibliography of their contents. Birmingham: Federation of Family History Societies, 1991. 2 vols.

**Scottish genealogist** [journal] Edinburgh: Scottish Genealogy Society, 1954–

## Latin and handwriting

**Gandy, Michael** Basic approach to Latin for family historians. Birmingham: Federation of Family History Societies, 1995.

**McLaughlin, Eve** Simple Latin for family historians. 5th ed. Birmingham: Federation of Family History Societies, 1994.

**Morris, Janet** A Latin glossary for family and local historians. Birmingham: Federation of Family History Societies, 1989.

**Simpson, Grant G.** Scottish handwriting 1150–1650: an introduction to the reading of documents. East Linton: Tuckwell Press, 1998.

**Stuart, Denis** Latin for local and family historians: a beginner's guide. Chichester: Phillimore, 1995.

## Occupations

*General*

**Raymond, S.** Occupational sources for genealogists: a bibliography. Birmingham: Federation of Family History Societies, 1992.

### Armed forces

#### Army
**Army** list. 1740, 1754– (annual).

**Fowler, Simon** Army records for family historians. London: Public Record Office, 1992.

**Fowler, Simon, Spencer, W. and Tamblin, S.** Army service records of the First World War. London: Public Record Office, 1996.

**Gibson, Jeremy and Medlycott, M.** Militia lists and musters 1757–1876. 2nd ed. Birmingham: Federation of Family History Societies, 1990.

**Hamilton-Edwards, Gerald** In search of army ancestry. London: Phillimore, 1977.

**Hart's** annual army list. 1840–1916 (annual).

**Holding, Norman** More sources of World War I army ancestry. 2nd ed. Birmingham: Federation of Family History Societies, 1991.

**Holding, Norman** World War I army ancestry. 2nd ed. Birmingham: Federation of Family History Societies, 1991.

**Swinnerton, Iain** The British army: its history, tradition and records. Birmingham: Federation of Family History Societies, 1996.

**Watts, M. J. and C. T.** My ancestor was in the British Army: how can I find out more about him? London: Society of Genealogists, 1992 (1995 reprint with addenda).

#### Royal Air Force
**Air** Force list. 1919–

**RAF** records in the PRO / Simon Fowler and others. London: Public Record Office, 1994.

**Wilson, Eunice** Records of the Royal Air Force: how to find The Few. Birmingham: Federation of Family History Societies, 1991.

#### Royal Marines
**Thomas, Garth** Records of the Royal Marines. London: Public Record Office, 1994.

*Royal Navy*

**Marshall, John** Royal Naval biography. London: Longman, [etc.], 1823–1835. 12 vols.

**Navy** list. 1814– (annual).

**New** navy list 1839–1855

**O'Byrne, William R.** A naval biographical dictionary. London: J. Murray, 1849.

**Rodger, N. A. M.** Naval records for genealogists. London: Public Record Office, 1984.

**Steel's** navy list. 1782–1817 (annual).


*Clergy*

The **Church** College in Aberdeen: Free Church College 1843–1900, United Free Church 1900–1929, complete roll of alumni 1843–1929. Aberdeen: Aberdeen University Press, 1930.

**Couper, William J.** The Reformed Presbyterian Church in Scotland, its congregations, ministers and students. Edinburgh: United Free Church of Scotland Publication Dept., 1925. [A Fasti of this Church from 1743–1876].

**Ewing, William** Annals of the Free Church of Scotland 1843–1900. Edinburgh: T. & T. Clark, 1914. 2 vols.

**Fasti** Ecclesiae Scoticanae: the succession of Ministers in the Church of Scotland from 1560. Edinburgh: Oliver & Boyd [various dates]. 9 vols.

**Fasti** Ecclesiae Scoticanae, vol. 10: ministers of the church from 1955–1975 / Donald F. Macleod Macdonald. Edinburgh: The Saint Andrew Press, 1981.

The **Fasti** of the United Free Church of Scotland, 1900–1929 / John A. Lamb. Edinburgh: Oliver & Boyd, 1956.

**Macgregor, William Malcolm and Blake, Buchanan** A historical sketch of the United Free Church College, Glasgow: with a complete alumnus roll from 1856 to 1929. Glasgow: 1930.

**MacKelvie, William** Annals & statistics of the United Presbyterian Church. Edinburgh: Oliphant & Co., 1873.

**Small, R.** History of the congregations of the United Presbyterian Church from 1733–1900. Edinburgh: David M. Small, 1904.

**United** Methodist ministers & their church / compiled by O. A. Beckerlegge. London: Epworth Press, 1968.

### Lawyers

The **Faculty** of Advocates in Scotland 1532–1943 with genealogical notes / edited by Sir Francis J. Grant. Edinburgh: Scottish Record Society, 1944.

**History** of the Society of Advocates in Aberdeen / edited by John Alexander Henderson. Aberdeen: New Spalding Club, 1912. [Includes a list of members 1549–1911 with biographical notes].

**History** of the Society of Writers to her Majesty's Signet ... with list of members ... from 1594 to 1890. Edinburgh: Society of Writers to her Majesty's Signet, 1890.

**Index** juridicus: the Scottish law list 1852– (annual)

The **Register** of the Society of Writers to the Signet. Edinburgh: Clark, Constable, 1983. [Details of members from the fifteenth century to the 1980s]

**Scottish** law list 1848–49.

### Medical and related professions

**Bourne, Susan and Chicken, Andrew H.** Records of the medical professions: a practical guide for the family historian. S. Bourne and A. H. Chicken, 1994.

**The Dentists** register 1879– (annual).

**Kelly's** directory of chemists and druggists 1869–1916 (annual) Some editions entitled: Post Office directory of chemists and druggists.

**London** & provincial medical directory 1861–1869.

**Medical** directory 1845– (annual).

**Medical** directory for Scotland 1852–1860.

**Medical** register 1859– (annual).

**The registers** of pharmaceutical chemists and chemists and druggists 1880–1953 (annual).

**Tough, A. G.** Medical archives of Glasgow and Paisley: a guide to the Greater Glasgow Health Board Archive. Glasgow: Wellcome Unit for the History of Medicine, University of Glasgow, 1993.

### Merchants and tradesmen

The **burgesses** & guild brethren of Glasgow, 1573–1750 / edited by James R. Anderson. Edinburgh: Scottish Record Society, 1923–1925.

The **burgesses** & guild brethren of Glasgow, 1751–1846 / edited by James R. Anderson. Edinburgh: Scottish Record Society, 1931–1935.

**Roll** of Edinburgh burgesses and guild-brethren, 1406–1700 / edited by Charles B. Boog Watson. Edinburgh: Scottish Record Society, 1926–1929.

**Roll** of Edinburgh burgesses and guild-brethren, 1701–1760 / edited by Charles B. Boog Watson. Edinburgh: Scottish Record Society, 1929–1930.

**Roll** of Edinburgh burgesses and guild-brethren, 1761–1841 / edited by Charles B. Boog Watson. Edinburgh: Scottish Record Society, 1933.

### Other occupations

**British** railways pre-grouping atlas and gazetteer. Shepperton: I. Allan, 1976.

**Loverseed, D. E.** Gasworker ancestors: how to find out more about them: a guide to genealogical sources for the British gas industry. Stockport: DCS, 1994.

**Richards, Tom** Was your grandfather a railwayman? 3rd ed. Bristol: T. Richards, 1995.

**Watts, M. J. and C. T.** My ancestor was a merchant seaman: how can I find out more about him? London: Society of Genealogists, 1991.

### Peerage and landed gentry

**Burke's** family index. London: Burke's Peerage, 1976.

**Burke's** genealogical and heraldic history of the peerage, baronetage and knightage. 105th ed. London: Burke's Peerage, 1970. 2 vols.

**Burke's** landed gentry. 18th ed. London: Burke's Peerage, 1965.

**Debrett's** peerage and baronetage. London: Debrett's Peerage, 1990.

**Paul, Sir James Balfour** The Scots peerage. Edinburgh: D. Douglas, 1904–1914. 9 vols.

### Recording and writing your family history

**Calder, A. and Lockwood, V.** Shooting video history: a video workshop on video recording for family and community historians, with accompanying notes. Milton Keynes: The Open University, 1993.

**Green H.** Projecting family history: a short guide to audio/visual construction. Plymouth: Federation of Family History Societies, 1979.

**Humphries, S. and Gordon, P.** Video memories: recording your family history. London: BBC Education, 1993.

**Lynskey, Marie** Family trees: a manual for their design, layout and display. Chichester: Phillimore, 1996.

**McLaughlin, Eve** Laying out a pedigree. Birmingham: Federation of Family History Societies, 1988.

**Palgrave-Moore, P. T. R.** How to record your family tree. 5th ed. Norwich: Elvery Dowers Publications, 1991.

**Phillimore, W. P. W.** How to write the history of a family. 2nd ed. London: Cupples and Hurd, 1888.

**Swinnerton, Iain** Basic facts about keeping your family records. Birmingham: Federation of Family History Societies, 1995.

**Templeton, Ian** Book success the family way. Pulborough, W. Sussex: Pikers' Pad, 1988.

**Templeton, Ian** How others write and publish family histories. Pulborough, W. Sussex: Pikers' Pad, 1989.

**Templeton, Ian** Publish it yourself and make it pay. Pulborough, W. Sussex: Pikers' Pad, 1993.

**Titford, John** Writing and publishing your family history. Birmingham: Federation of Family History Societies, 1996.

## Specific sources

### Census records

**Census** returns, 1841–1891 in microfilm: a directory to local holdings / by Jeremy Gibson and Elizabeth Hampson. 6th ed. Birmingham: Federation of Family History Societies, 1994.

**Census** returns and old parochial registers on microfilm: a directory of public library holdings in the West of Scotland / compiled by Anne Escott. Rev. ed. Glasgow: Glasgow District Libraries, 1986.

**Dewdney, J. C.** The British census. Norwich: Geo Books, 1981. (Concepts and techniques in modern geography; no. 29).

**Gibson, Jeremy and Medlycott, M.** Local census listings, 1522–1930: holdings in the British Isles. Birmingham: Federation of Family History Societies, 1992.

**Gibson, Jeremy and Hampson, Elizabeth** Marriage, census and other indexes for family historians. 6th ed. Birmingham: Federation of Family History Societies, 1996.

**Higgs, Edward** A clearer sense of the census: the Victorian censuses and historical research. London: HMSO, 1996.

**Johnson, Gordon** Census records for Scottish families at home and abroad. 2nd ed. Aberdeen: Aberdeen & North East Scotland Family History Society, 1994.

**Ruthven-Murray, P.** Scottish census indexes, covering the 1841–1871 civil censuses. Aberdeen: Scottish Association of Family History Societies, 1996.

*International Genealogical Index (I. G. I.) and Family Search (CD-ROM version of I. G. I.)*

**McLaughlin, Eve** Making the most of the IGI. 3rd ed. The author, 1995.

**Nichols, Elizabeth L.** Genealogy in the computer age: understanding FamilySearch. Rev. ed. Salt Lake City, Utah: Family History Educators, 1994.

*Newspapers*

**Ferguson, Joan P. S.**
Directory of Scottish newspapers / compiled by Miss Joan P. S. Ferguson. Edinburgh: National Library of Scotland, 1984.

**Glasgow** Herald index 1906–1984

**McLaughlin, Eve** Family history from newspapers. 2nd ed. Aylesbury, Bucks.: Varneys Press, 1994.

*Nonconformist records*

**Breed, G. R.** My ancestors were Baptists: how can I find out more about them? 3rd rev. ed. London: Society of Genealogists, 1995.

**Gandy, Michael** Catholic family history: a bibliography for Scotland. Aberdeen: Scottish Association of Family History Societies, 1996.

**Gandy, Michael** Catholic missions and registers 1700–1880, vol. 6: Scotland. London: M. Gandy, 1993.

**Leary, W.** My ancestors were Methodists: how can I find out more about them? 2nd ed. London: Society of Genealogists, 1990.

**Milligan, E. H. and Thomas, M. J.** My ancestors were Quakers: how can I find out more about them? London: Society of Genealogists, 1990.

**Mordy, I.** My ancestors were Jewish: how can I find out more about them? London: Society of Genealogists, 1995.

**National** Index of Parish Registers, vol. 2: sources for nonconformist genealogy and family history / edited by D. J. Steel. London: Society of Genealogists, 1972.

**National** Index of Parish Registers, vol. 3: sources for Roman Catholic and Jewish genealogy and family history / by D. J. Steel and E. R. Samuel. London: Society of Genealogists, 1973.

*Photographs*

**Family** history in focus / edited by D. Steel and L. Taylor. Guildford: Lutterworth Press, 1984.

**Linkman, A.** Caring for your family photographs at home. Manchester: Documentary Photography Archive, 1991.

**Oliver, George** Photographs and local history. London: Batsford, 1989.

**Pols, Robert** Dating old photographs. 2nd ed. Birmingham: Federation of Family History Societies, 1995.

*Wills*

**Camp, A. J.** Wills and their whereabouts. Canterbury: Phillimore, 1974.

**The Commissariot** record of [various Commissariots]. Register of testaments. Edinburgh: Scottish Record Society, 1897–1904. [Indexes of testaments to 1800].

**Gibson, Jeremy** Probate jurisdictions: where to look for wills. 4th ed. Birmingham: Federation of Family History Societies, 1993.

**Gibson, Jeremy** Wills and where to find them. London: Phillimore, 1974.

**Index** to the Prerogative Wills of Ireland, 1536–1810 / edited by Sir Arthur Vicars. Dublin: E. Ponsonby, 1897.

*Other specific sources*

**Census** returns and old parochial registers on microfilm: a directory of public library holdings in the West of Scotland / compiled by Anne Escott. Rev. ed. Glasgow: Glasgow District Libraries, 1986.

**"Claverhouse" (M. C. Smith)** Irregular Border marriages. Edinburgh: Moray Press, 1934.

**Gibson, Jeremy and Rogers, C.** Electoral registers since 1832; and burgess rolls. Birmingham: Federation of Family History Societies, 1993.

**Gibson, Jeremy and Hampson, Elizabeth** Marriage, census and other indexes for family historians. 6th ed. Birmingham: Federation of Family History Societies, 1996.

**Gouldesbrough, Peter** Formulary of old Scots legal documents. Edinburgh: Stair Society, 1985.

**Litton, Pauline with Chapman, Colin** Basic facts about using marriage records for family historians. Birmingham: Federation of Family History Societies, 1996.

**Litton, Pauline** Using baptism records. Birmingham: Federation of Family History Societies, 1996.

**McLaughlin, Eve** Interviewing elderly relatives. 2nd ed. Plymouth: Federation of Family History Societies, 1985.

**Poll** books c1696–1872: a directory to holdings in Great Britain / by Jeremy Gibson and Colin Rogers. 3rd ed. Birmingham: Federation of Family History Societies, 1994.

**Probert, Eric D.** Company and business records for family historians. Birmingham: Federation of Family History Societies, 1994.

**Shaw, G. and Tipper, A.** British directories: a bibliography and guide to directories published in England and Wales, 1850–1950; and Scotland, 1773–1950. Leicester: Leicester University Press, 1989.

**Swinnerton, Iain** Basic facts about sources for family history in the home. Birmingham: Federation of Family History Societies, 1995.

**Timperley, Loretta R.** A directory of landownership in Scotland, c.1770. Edinburgh: Scottish Record Society, 1976.

## Study of genealogy

**Family** history at the crossroads: a Journal of family history reader / edited by Tamara Hareven and Andrejs Plakans. Princeton, N. J.: Princeton University Press, 1987.

**Ryan, Gerald H. and Redstone, Lilian J.** Timperley of Hintlesham: a study of a Suffolk family. London: Methuen, 1931.

**Sayers, S.** 'The psychological significance of genealogy', in Perspectives on contemporary legend / edited by G. Bennett, P. Smith and J. D. A. Widdowson. Sheffield: Sheffield University Press, 1987.

**Wagner, Sir Anthony** English ancestry. London: Oxford University Press, 1961.

**Wagner, Sir Anthony** English genealogy. 3rd ed. Chichester: Phillimore, 1983.

**Wagner, Sir Anthony** Pedigree and progress. London: Phillimore, 1975.

### Surnames

**Black, George F.** The surnames of Scotland: their origin, meaning and history. New York: New York Public Library, 1946. (Reprinted: – Edinburgh: Birlinn, 1993.)

**Hanks, Patrick and Hodges, Flavia** A dictionary of surnames. Oxford: Oxford University Press, 1990.

**McKinley, Richard** A history of British surnames. London: Longman, 1990.

**Rogers, Colin** The surname detective. Manchester: Manchester University Press, 1995.

# Index

Aberdeen, 56
Aberdeen University, 6, 57
Aberdeenshire, 53
Acadian genealogy, 105
Adam and Eve, 7
Advocates, 56
Aelfwine, Sheriff of
    Warwickshire, 10
Aeneas, 7
Aggregation, 5–6
Ancestry, factors in tracing, 8–10
Apprenticeship, 72, 77, 78
Arden family, 10
Argyll, Dukes of, estate
    collections, 80
Aristotle, 7
Army, 48, 49
Asclepius, God of medicine, 7
Audio cassettes, 38, 39
Auxiliary Forces Associations, 50

Bach family, 4
Banffshire, 53
Bank of Scotland, 51
Bankruptcies, 51
Baptisms, 64–65, 74–75, 80–82
Baptist Church, 75
Bards, 7–8
Bible, 7
Biographical dictionaries, 60–62
Birth briefs, 19, 21, 22
Birth certificates, 14, 25
Births, marriages and deaths,
    24–27, 31–32, 103
    indexes, 32
Bounties, 78
Brock, John, 77
Brock, Robert, 78
Brock, William (Junior), 77–78

Brock, William (Senior), 78
Burgesses, 77
Burgh records, 46, 52, 70–71,
    72–73, 74, 76, 77, 78
Burials, 64–65, 74–75, 80–81
Businesses, 51

Cambridge Group for the History
    of Population and Social
    Structure, 5
CD–ROMs, 32–33, 52, 60
Cemeteries, 67
Census records, 24, 26, 27–32,
    37–38, 43, 97, 103
    indexes, 28, 32
Charlemagne, Emperor, 12
Chemists, 55
China, 7
Church account books, 45
Church Courts, 68
Church members, 45, 74–75
Church of Jesus Christ of Latter
    Day Saints, 4, 32–33, 36
    libraries, 33, 65–66
Church of Scotland, 45, 73, 74
Church of Scotland Ministers,
    51–52
Circular family trees, 21, 23
Civil Registers, 24–27, 31–32
    indexes, 32, 103
Clans, Japanese, 7
    Scottish, 7–8, 9, 98, 103
Clergymen, 51–52
Coal miners, 47–48
Commissary Courts, 68–69, 73
Computers, 35–38, 82
Congregational Church, 75
Constantine VII, Byzantine
    Emperor, 12

Continuous Service Engagement Books, 49
Conway, Margaret, 47
County Council records, 46, 50, 53
Court of Session, 56, 72–73
Craft guilds, 77
Crew lists, 50–51

Databases, 37–38, 102–103
Deacons Court minutes, 53
Death certificates, 14, 26–27
Deeds, Registers of, 72–73
Demography, historical, 5–6, 82–83
Dentists, 55
Destitution Boards, 46–47
Dick Bequest Trust, 53
Dick, James, 53
Directories, genealogical, 91–92
Directories, street and trade, 43–45
Disruption of 1843, 74
District Council records, 46
Doctors, 54–55
Dougall, John, 2, 44–45, 54, 57, 61–62
Dougall, John McPhail, 57
Drop line charts, 19, 20
Dudley, Barony of, 11
Dunbartonshire, Sasines, 71
Duncan, Agnes, 78
Duncan, John, 78
Dundas, Helias de, 10
Dundas family, 10
Dundee, 10, 97

E–mail, 99–102
Economic history, 5, 6
Edinburgh, 10, 41–42, 43–44, 51, 74, 77, 97
    Central Library, 42, 59
    Commissariot, 69
    Diocese of (Episcopal), 80
    National Library of Scotland, 80
    National Register of Archives (Scotland), 51, 75, 77, 79–80, 103
    New Register House, 24, 28, 31–32, 33, 65, 94, 103

Royal College of Physicans of Edinburgh, 55
Royal College of Surgeons of Edinburgh, 55
Royal High School Athletic Club, Rugby Section, 80
Scottish Genealogy Society, 67, 104
Scottish Record Office **see** Scottish Record Office
University, 57
West Register House, 80
Educational Institute of Scotland (EIS), 53
Educational sources, 56–58
Edward I, 12
Electoral Registers, 42
Elizabeth, Queen Mother, 11
Emigration, 97
England and Wales, 93–95
    Administrations, 94
    Births, marriages and deaths, 27, 93–94
    Census records, 94
    Civil Registers, 27, 93–94
    Family Records Centre, London, 94
    International Genealogical Index (IGI), 94
    Land records, 95
    Manorial Court Rolls, 95
    Marriage licences, 94-95
    Parish Registers, 94
    Wills, 94
Episcopal Church of Scotland, 75, 80
Estate papers, 79, 80
Eugenics, 4
Everton's genealogical helper, 105–106

Family gatherings, 39
Family histories, 59
Family history, writing, 84–90
Family history societies, 93
Family reconstitution, 6, 82
Family Records Centre, London, 94
Family Search, 33
Family traditions, 1–2

Family trees, 16, 19–23
Federation of Family History
    Societies, 93
Fife, Sasines, 72
Fishing, 78
Free Church of Scotland, 53,
    74, 75
    Deacons Court minutes, 53
    schools, 53

Galton, Sir Francis, 4
Genealogical directories, 91–92
Genealogy, study of, 7–8
Genetics, 4
GENUKI, 104
GENUKI-L, 99–100
Gifts and Deposits Collections
    (SRO), 48, 50, 73, 79
Gifts and Deposits Textbase,
    79, 103
Glasgow, 2, 6, 10, 11, 41–42,
    43–44, 47, 61, 64, 71, 74, 75,
    77, 97
    Archdiocese of (Roman
        Catholic), 75
    City Archives, 2, 42, 47, 51,
        71, 75, 97–103
    *Glasgow Herald* newspaper, 59
    Jordanhill College of
        Education, 58
    Mitchell Library, 42, 59
    Registers of Scotland,
        Cowglen, 71
    Registrar's Office, Park
        Circus, 32
    Royal College of Physicians
        and Surgeons of
        Glasgow, 55
    Royal Infirmary, 61
    Scottish Brewing Archive, 51,
        103
    University of Glasgow, 6,
        57–58
    University of Glasgow
        Archives, 51, 103
    University of Strathclyde,
        6, 42
    University of Strathclyde,
        Faculty of Education, 58
Gravestones, 66–67
Gray, Margaret, 47

Guilds, 77

Hamilton, Dukes of, estate
    collections, 80
Health Boards, 55
Hearth Tax, 76–77
Henry VII, 11
Henry VIII, 12
Heritors records, 46, 52, 74
Herring fishing, 78
Hicks, Anthony, 11
Highlands and Islands, 46–47, 53
Hintlesham, Suffolk,
    Manor of, 11
Hippocrates, 7
Historical demography, 5–6,
    82–83
Holton family, 11
Holton, Laura Elizabeth, 45
Hospitals
    patients, 55
    staff, 55
Howard family, Dukes of
    Norfolk, 11
Howard, Margaret, 11
Howard, Thomas, 3rd Duke of
    Norfolk, 11–12
Hulson family, 92

Identification, 80–83
IGI, 32–33, 38, 65, 94
Immigration, 97–98
Incorporations, 77
Indentures of apprenticeship, 78
Industrial Revolution, 9–10
Inherited diseases, 4
International Genealogical Index
    (IGI), 32–33, 38, 65, 94
Internet, 98–106
Ireland
    Administrations, 96
    Births, marriages and deaths, 95
    Census records, 95
    Church of Ireland registers, 96
    Civil registers, 95
    Genealogical Office, Dublin, 96
    General Register Office
        (Northern Ireland),
        Belfast, 95
    General Register Office of
        Ireland, Dublin, 95

Land records, 97
Marriage licences, 96–97
Monumental inscriptions, 97
National Archives, Dublin,
    95, 96, 97, 104
National Library of Ireland,
    Dublin, 96
North of Ireland Family
    History Society, 104
Presbyterian Church
    registers, 96
Presbyterian Historical Society,
    Belfast, 96
Protestant Church registers, 95
Public Record Office of
    Northern Ireland, 96, 104
Register of Deeds, 97
Registry of Deeds, Dublin, 97
Roman Catholic Church
    registers, 96
Wills, 95, 96
Irish immigrants, 10, 47, 97

Japan, 7
    clans, 7
Jordanhill College of
    Education, 58
Journals for family historians, 92
Julius Caesar, 7
Justices of the Peace, 78

Kinning Park, 45, 61
Kirk Session records, 46, 52,
    73–74

Land ownership, 69–72, 76
Land records, 69–72, 76
Landed gentry, 61
Laslett, Peter, 5
Lawyers, 56
Leaving certificate, 57
Licensees, 78
Lister, Joseph, 61
Literacy, 5
Local archives, 45, 46, 51, 52, 53,
    56, 67, 68, 71, 73, 74, 77, 78,
    79–80, 94, 95
Local Courts, 73
Local government elections, 42–43
Local histories, 59
Local history, 5

London, 45
McArthur, Duncan, 1–2, 61
McArthur, Duncan, gardener, 2
McArthur, Florence, 2, 64
McPhail, John, Greenock mail-
    coach guard, 44, 64
Magazines for family historians,
    92
Margaret of France, 12
Margaret of Scotland, St., 12
Marriage certificates, 14, 25–26
Marriage contracts, 72
Marriages, 64–65, 74–75, 80–82
Memorial University,
    Newfoundland, 51
Merchant seamen, 50–51, 78
Methodist Church, 75
Militia, 50
Ministers (of religion), 51–52
Ministry of Defence, 50
Mitchell Library, 42, 59
Monumental inscriptions, 66–67
Morayshire, 53
Mormon Church, 4, 32–33, 36
    libraries, 33, 65–66
Mowbray family, Dukes of
    Norfolk, 11–12
Munnings, Sir Alfred, 2
Munnings, Sarah Green, 2
Munnings, William Green, 2
Musical biography, 61
Muster Books and Pay Lists, 50
Mutual Benefit Societies, 78

Names, 8–9, 82
National Coal Board, 47–48
National Library of Scotland, 80
National Maritime Museum,
    London, 51
National Register of Archives, 103
National Register of Archives
    (Scotland), 51, 75, 77, 79–80,
    103
National Register of Archives
    (Scotland)Textbase, 80, 103
Navy, 48, 49
New Register House, 24, 28,
    31–32, 33, 65, 94
Newhaven, 29, 31
Newsgroups, 99–102
Newspapers, 58–59

Nobility, 61
Nonconformist records, 45,
    51–52, 63–64, 74–75
Normans, 10
North British Railway Company, 48
Nurses, 55

Obituaries, 58
Oral history, 89
Ordnance Survey maps, 41
Orkney, Wills and Testaments,
    68

Parish Councils, 46
Parish Registers, 24, 33, 63–66,
    103
Parks Departments, 67
Parochial Boards, 46
Patronymics, 9
Peerage, 61
Personal Ancestral File (PAF),
    36–37
Poll Tax, 76–77
Poor Law records, 46–47
Poor relief, 73–74
Poor Relief Applications,
    46–47, 97
Poor Relief Applications database,
    47, 97
Prerogative Court of Canterbury
    Wills, 94
Presbytery Minute Books, 52
Proclamations of banns of
    marriage, 64–65
Public Record Office, London,
    48, 49, 50, 51, 97, 104–105
Publicans, 78

Quaker Church, 75

Railwaymen, 48
Ramsay family, 29, 31, 101
RAND Genealogy Club, 106
Recording information, 17–18,
    34–39
Reform Acts, 42
Register House, 24, 28, 31–32,
    33, 65, 94, 104
Registers of Deeds, 72–73
Registers of Scotland, Cowglen,
    Glasgow, 71

Registers of Seamen's Services,
    49
Registrar's Office, Park Circus,
    Glasgow, 32
Relatives, interviewing, 15–18
Renfrewshire, Sasines, 71
Retours, or Services of Heirs,
    69–70
Roman Catholic Church, 63–64,
    75
ROOTS surnames list, 101–102
Roxburghe, Dukes of, estate
    collections, 80
Royal Air Force, 50
Royal Bank of Scotland, 51
Royal College of Physicians and
    Surgeons of Glasgow, 55
Royal College of Physicians of
    Edinburgh, 55
Royal College of Surgeons of
    Edinburgh, 55
Royal Commission on Historical
    Manuscripts, 105
Royal Flying Corps, 50
Royal High School Athletic Club,
    Edinburgh. Rugby Section, 80
Royal Naval Air Service, 50

St. Andrews University, 57
St. Margaret of Scotland, 12
St. Mungo College, 61
Salt Lake City, U.S.A., 4
Sasines, 70–72, 76, 95, 97
Scanning (computer), 37
Schofield, R.S., 5
School Boards, 53
School pupils, 56–57
School teachers, 52–53
Schools, 52–53
    admission registers, 56
    log books, 56
    pupils, 56–57
    teachers, 52–53
Scottish Brewing Archive, 51
Scottish Episcopal Church, 75
    Congregations in the Diocese
    of Edinburgh, 80
Scottish Genealogy Society, 67,
    104
Scottish Record Office (SRO), 41,
    43, 45, 46, 47, 48, 51, 52, 53,

55, 56, 57, 67, 68, 69, 70, 71, 73, 74, 75, 76, 77, 78, 79, 80, 94, 103
Sennachies, 7–8
Services of heirs, 69–70
Shaen, Richard, 58
Sheriff Court records, 46, 50, 69, 72–73
Shetland, Wills and Testaments, 68
Ship passenger lists, 97
Ships' musters, 49
Social history, 4–6
Social mobility, 10–12
Society in Scotland for Propagating Christian Knowledge (SSPCK), 53
Society of Free Fishermen of Newhaven, 78
Society of Genealogists, 105
Software, genealogical, 36–37
Soldiers' Documents, 50
Solicitors, 56
Somerset House, London, 95
Stamp duty, 64
Statistical Accounts of Scotland, 89
Strathclyde University, 6, 42
Strathclyde University, Faculty of Education, 58
Street directories, 43–45
Suffolk, 11
Surgeons, 54–55
Surnames, 8–9

Tape–recorders, 16, 17, 38, 89
Tape/slide presentations, 89–90
Tennant's Works, St. Rollox, 62
Territorial Army, 50
Testaments, 67–69, 72
Thomas of Brotherton, 12
Timperley, Sarah, 11

Timperley, Thomas, 11
Timperley, William, 11
Trade directories, 43–45
Trades, 77–78
Trafalgar, Battle of, 1–2

Unitarian Church, 75
United Presbyterian Church of Scotland, 75
Universities, 54–55, 80
Aberdeen, 6, 57
Edinburgh, 57
Glasgow, 6, 57–58
Glasgow, Archives, 51
St. Andrews, 57
Strathclyde, 6, 42
Strathclyde, Faculty of Education, 58
students, 57–58

Valuation Roll Index, 42
Valuation Rolls, 41–42, 76
Venus, Goddess, 7
*Victory,* H.M.S., 1–2
Video recordings, 38–39, 89–90
Volunteer Forces, 50
Voters Rolls **see** Electoral Registers

Wages books, 79
Wagner, Sir Anthony, 8
Wards (electoral), 43
West Register House, 80
Whaling, 78
William the Conqueror, 10, 12
Williamsburgh, 30
Wills, 67–69
Women voters, 42–43
Word processing, 37
World Wide Web, 102–106
Wrigley, E.A., 5, 82
Writers to the Signet, 56